CLASSROOM PARTIES

Thanks to Janice and Joel for sharing their office with me.

CLASSROOM PARTIES

By:
Susan Spaete

Art:
Rick Abbott
Bill Peck

A BUILDING BLOCKS Publication

© 1987 by Liz and Dick Wilmes

ISBN 0-943452-07-4

All rights reserved. No part of this publication may be reproduced, stored in a retrieval system, or transmitted, in any form, or by any means, electronic, mechanical, photocopying or otherwise except for the inclusion of brief quotations in a review, without prior written permission of the publisher. Printed in the United States of America.

COVER CONSULTANTS:
    Pat and Greg Samata
    Samata Associates, Inc.
    Dundee, Illinois 60118

PUBLISHED BY:
    BUILDING BLOCKS
    38W567 Brindlewood
    Elgin, Illinois 60123

DISTRIBUTED BY:
    GRYPHON HOUSE, Inc.
    P.O. Box 275
    Mt. Rainier, Maryland 20712

ISBN 0-943452-07-4
$8.95

Dedicated to

. . . children and adults laughing and playing together.

CONTENTS

Dedication

FALL

First Day of School 9
Columbus Day 15
Halloween Party 22
Thanksgiving Party 29

WINTER

Hanukkah Party 35
Christmas Party 40
Martin Luther King, Jr. Day 47
Groundhog's Day 52
Valentine Party 57
Presidents' Day 64
St. Patrick's Day 70

SPRING

Easter 77
April Fools Day 84
Arbor Day 89
May Day 94

SUMMER

Patriotic Days 99
Birthday and a Half 104
Good-bye Party 107

YOUR FAVORITE PARTY IDEAS

Favorite Themes 111
Favorite Snacks 112
Favorite Games 113
Favorite Songs and Rhymes 114

● ● ●

FIRST DAY OF SCHOOL

SPECIAL PARTY TIME

About two weeks before the first day of school send a letter to each of the children. In the letter welcome them and tell them the necessary information they need to know for the first day. In the last paragraph tell the children a little about yourself and include a photo. Tell them that on the first day of school they should each bring a photo of themselves. They should also think of one thing they would like to tell the others, such as something about their families, a vacation they took, a pet, etc.

On the first day have a bulletin board ready to display all of the photos. At the first circle time give each child the opportunity to hold up his photo, tell his name and one other thing he'd like to share. After he's had this time, help him tack his photo to the bulletin board. Add his name under the photo.

CIRCLE TIME

Quiet Games

• HERE I AM — Take some time in the beginning of the session to see who is there. Use a special puppet to sing a "Hello" song to everyone.

HELLO
(tune: Where Is Thumbkin?)

Puppet asks — *Where is (Child's Name)?*
                Where is (Child's Name)?

Child answers — *Here I am. Here I am.*

Puppet asks — *How are you today, (Child's Name)?*
                How are you today, (Child's Name)?

Child answers — *I am fine* (well, happy, sad or whatever he chooses.)*! I am fine!*

Puppet says — *Good-bye now! Good-bye now!*

Continue the song for each child.

• COLOR CARDS — Give each of the children a red, yellow, blue, green, purple, and orange card. Have them lay the cards in front of them. Say each color and have the children point to the appropriate card. Then give them directions:

— *"Find your red card, hold it up, and lay it on your head."* (Put it back.)

— *"Find the yellow card and sit on it."* (Put it back.)

— *"Find the green card and balance it on your knee."* (Put it back.)

— *"Find the purple card and lay it on one of your feet."* (Put it back.)

— *"Find the orange card and balance it on your nose."* (Put it back.)

• CLASSROOM GUIDELINES — Using the special puppet, talk with the children about walking in the classroom, using quiet voices, being kind to one another, where the washroom is, what the general schedule is, and so on.

Active Games

• TOUR THE ROOM — Take a walk around the classroom showing the children the different areas, what to do in the areas, and any special instructions they need to know. As you are leading the children remind them of safety, cleanliness, and courtesy to others.

• CALL BALL — Have the children sit in a circle with a small beachball. Say a child's name and roll it to him. He can say another child's name or your name and roll it to that person. Continue rolling the ball around the circle remembering to say names first.

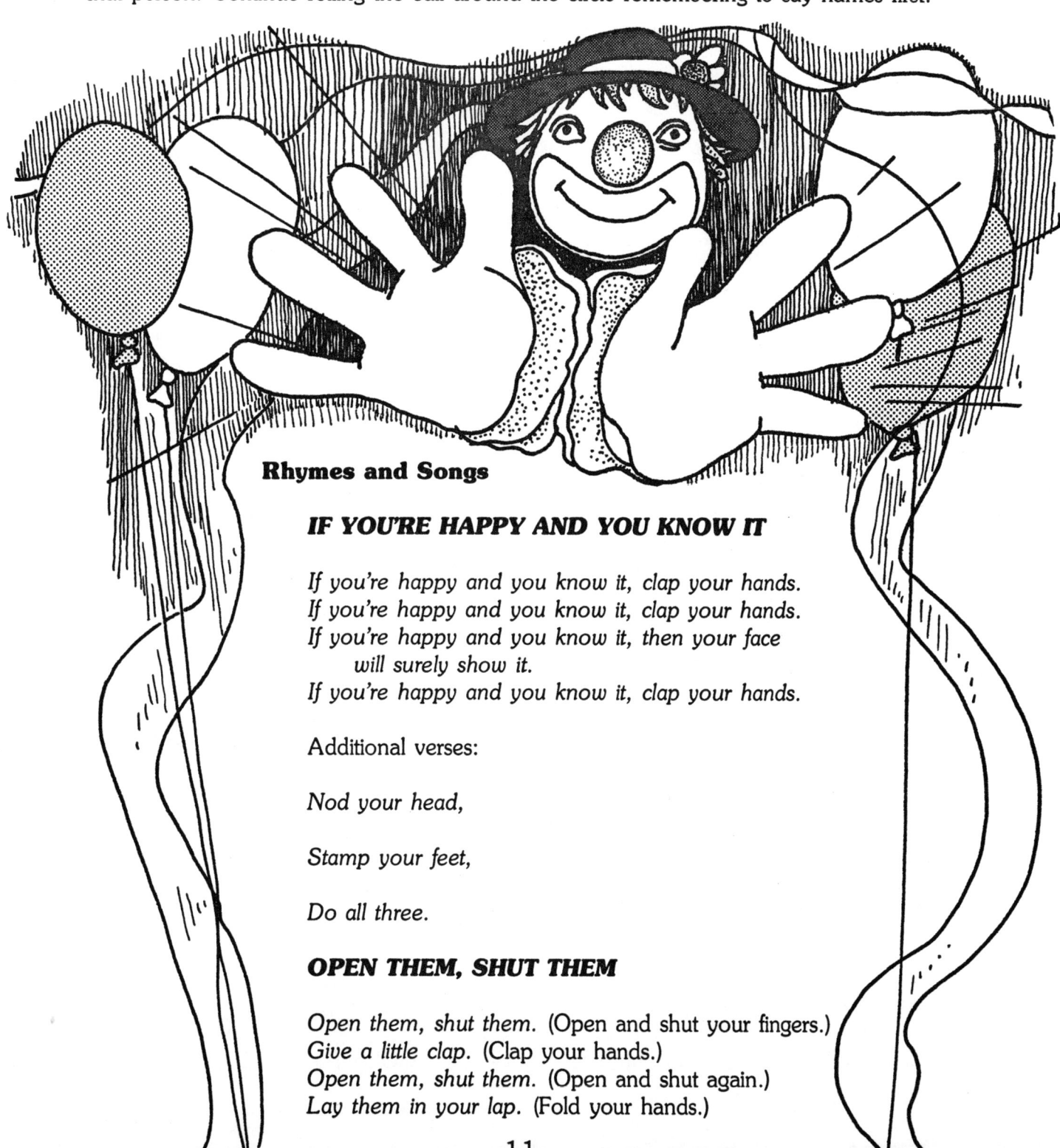

Rhymes and Songs

IF YOU'RE HAPPY AND YOU KNOW IT

If you're happy and you know it, clap your hands.
If you're happy and you know it, clap your hands.
*If you're happy and you know it, then your face
   will surely show it.*
If you're happy and you know it, clap your hands.

Additional verses:

Nod your head,

Stamp your feet,

Do all three.

OPEN THEM, SHUT THEM

Open them, shut them. (Open and shut your fingers.)
Give a little clap. (Clap your hands.)
Open them, shut them. (Open and shut again.)
Lay them in your lap. (Fold your hands.)

11

NEW FRIENDS

*So many children
It's going to be fun.
They know their own names,
But I only know one.*
          by Dick Wilmes

CLEAN UP TIME

*It's clean up time in the school
It's time for girls and boys
To stop what they are doing now
And put away their toys.*

Explain that they must put everything away. Help them when necessary.

Story Time

• Read BEST FRIENDS by Miriam Cohen or SHAWN GOES TO SCHOOL by Petronella Breinburg.

ACTIVITY TIME

Art

• FIRST DAY NECKLACES — Have the children paint paper plates any color they would like. When the plates are dry have the children each tell you one thing they like about school. Ask them if you could write what they liked on the backsides of their plates. (Do it if they agree.) Punch two holes in each of the plates, loop them with yarn and give them to the children to wear as necklaces.

• SOFT DOUGH — Make a fresh batch of soft dough for the children to roll, poke, form, mold, and stretch.

SOFT DOUGH

You'll Need:

4 cups of flour
1 cup salt
2 T vegetable oil
4 T alum
3 cups boiling water
Food coloring (optional)

To Make: Mix the first four ingredients in a large bowl. Add food coloring to the boiling water if you want colored dough. Pour the water into the bowl. Stir until cooled down and then put on the counter. Knead until smooth. Store in an airtight container.

Cooking

CHEESE SNACKS

You'll Need:

Cheese slices

To Make: Let the children use table knives and cut pieces of cheese. Put them on a plate and cover them until snack time.

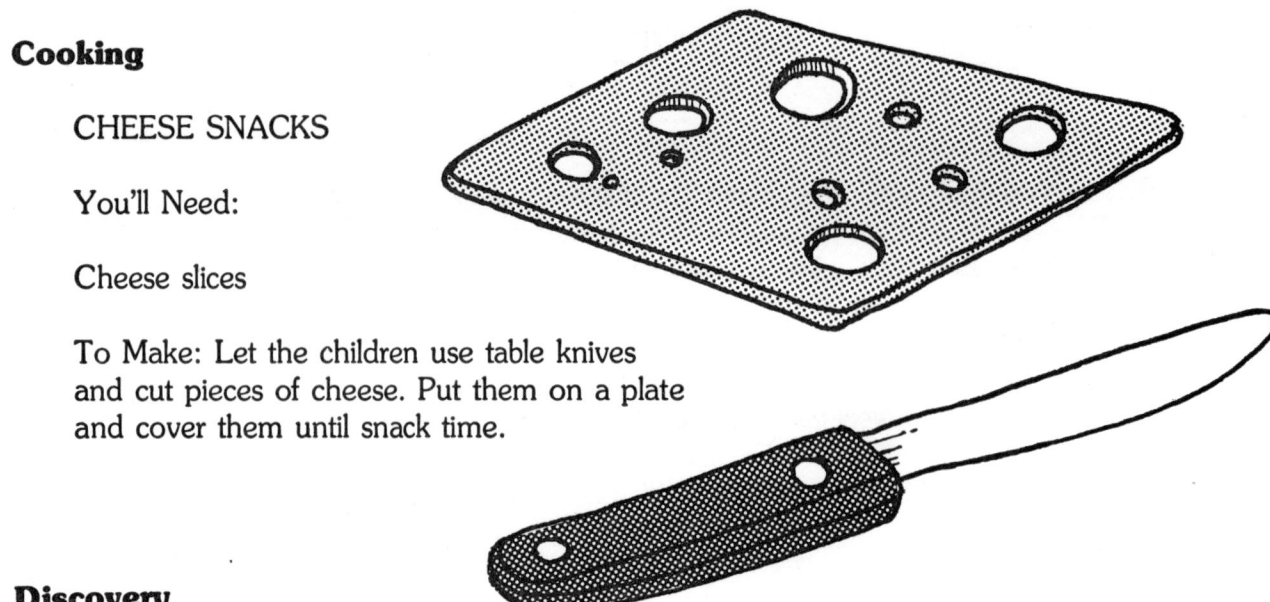

Discovery

• BEACH ITEMS — Have a display of things the children might find at a beach — several types of sand, rocks, shells, and seaweed. Have a magnifying glass so they can examine the objects more closely.

SNACK TIME

Snack

• Have different shaped crackers and the plate of cheese the children cut. Serve with glasses of juice. Talk about the shapes of the crackers as everyone eats.

DISMISSAL TIME

Talk with the children about all of the things they did in school. Teach them this chant and then let them tell one favorite activity.

*Children, children what do you say
Which was your favorite activity today?*

COLUMBUS DAY

SPECIAL PARTY TIME

Have the children act out a simple version of the story of Christopher Columbus as you, pretending to be Columbus, tell it.

"The King and Queen of Spain just gave me enough money to sail to a new world. I need to get my three ships, the Nina, Pinta, and Santa Maria. I will hire lots of sailors and get the necessary food. Who would like to be one of my sailors? (All of the children who want to be a sailor raise their hands. Give each child a sailor cap.) *All of us are ready to sail. Climb into one of the ships.* (Roughly divide the children into three groups for sailing in the three ships.)

All ready mates? Begin to row. (All of the sailors row until they get out to sea.) *OK, let's put up the sails.* (Have the children hoist the sails.) *It's getting dark now. Half of you sailors can sleep while the other half must stay awake to sail the ships.* (Half pretend to sleep. In a little while switch.) *At night we must be extra careful not to get lost. Watch the stars and the moon.* (Children look up at the stars and moon.) *The sun is rising. It is beautiful. Oh, the ocean is getting very rough. There is a storm. It's very bumpy. Look at the huge waves.* (Children jostle around.) *I hope the storm settles down!* (Finally it does.)

I hope we can see land pretty soon. (Have several children cup their hands into telescopes and look for land.) *I see birds. That means land must be very close.* (Everyone looks for land.) *Look, there are trees waving in the breeze.* (Everyone agrees.) *Land! Land!* (Have the children row up to the land and get out of the ships.) *Let us say a prayer of thanks and put the flag of Spain in the ground."* (Have a Spanish flag and pass it to all of the children and then stand it in a piece of styrofoam. Everyone shouts 'Hurray! Hurray!')

CIRCLE TIME

Quiet Game

• DISCUSSING TRIPS — Talk with the children about taking trips. Let them tell each other about places they have gone. Include what they took on their trips, where they stayed, what they did, and so on.

• SHAPE OF THE WORLDS — Have a book, a sphere, and a small model boat to show the children. Tell them that about 500 years ago the people who were living thought that the world was flat. If a ship would sail it would fall off the edge. (Demonstrate.) Columbus along with others thought the world was round, so that when they sailed on the ocean they would not fall off the edge. (Demonstrate.) Columbus persuaded the King and Queen of Spain to give him ships and money to prove this and to reach the treasures of India.

• ANCHORS AWAY — Give each child a piece of flat styrofoam and a toothpick to construct a ship for the game. Have them insert the toothpick into the styrofoam. Ask each of them which ship they made, the Nina, Pinta, or Santa Maria.

Have small bowls of Cheerios® for the children to use to build their sails. Say a number. Each child takes that many Cheerios® from the bowl closest to him and slips them onto his toothpick. Continue adding Cheerios® until the sails are full. When they're full, it's time to sail. Encourage the children to sail their ships for awhile.

• SHAPE HUNT — Show the children a sphere shape and something that is flat. Pass each around. Now hold up the sphere. Tell the children to walk around the room and hunt for something that is that shape. When they find it they should stand by it. Let each child tell what he has found. Repeat by asking the children to find flat objects like counter and shelf tops.

Active Games

- GO SHIPS — Before playing this game talk with the children about how different water vehicles move — sailboats by sails, row boats by oars, motorboats by engines, rafts by poles, etc.

  To play, tell the children what type of water vehicle they will be. When you say *"Go ships,"* the children should pretend to be driving that type of vehicle. If their vehicle makes noise they can also make the sound. When you say *"Stop ships,"* they should all stop. Switch to another type of vehicle and play again. To extend this game use other forms of transportation.

- DISCOVER THE NEW WORLD — Cut out large star shapes from construction paper. Tape them to the floor in a long maze. At the end of the maze put a globe.

  To play, tell the children that they are going to pretend to be Christopher Columbus sailing his ship at night. (Turn off the lights and close the curtains to darken the room slightly.) They will follow the stars just as he did. Beginning at the first star have the children walk and row along the path until they reach the New World.

  When they have all landed, show the children the shape of the world and maybe the path Columbus followed across the ocean.

Rhymes and Songs

COLUMBUS SAILED
(tune: Michael Rowed the Boat Ashore.)

Columbus sailed in three ships, Allelluia.
Columbus sailed in three ships, Allelluia.

He sailed his ships in 1492, Allelluia.
He sailed his ships in 1492, Allelluia.

He knew the world was a sphere, Allelluia.
He knew the world was a sphere, Allelluia.

He discovered the New Land, Allelluia.
He discovered the New Land, Allelluia.

He claimed the land for the king and queen, Allelluia.
He claimed the land for the king and queen, Allelluia.

(May continue by asking the children what they would like to travel in . . . use their name and transportation in the song.)

THREE LITTLE SHIPS

Columbus sailed in ships of wood
On the Nina, the Pinta, and the Santa Maria.
He didn't fall off the earth as they said he would
On the Nina, the Pinta, and the Santa Maria.

He found several islands which were warm and green
On the Nina, the Pinta, and the Santa Maria.
And claimed the new land for the King and Queen
On the Nina, the Pinta, and the Santa Maria.

by Dick Wilmes

(Variation: The adult says lines one and three in each stanza and the children chant two and four.)

Story

• Read the children a story about boats. You might choose SONG OF THE BOATS by Lorenz Graham.

ACTIVITY TIME

Art

• STYROFOAM SHIPS — Have styrofoam squares, crayons, scissors, toothpicks, and construction paper available.

Have the children cut out and decorate sails for their ships. Help them insert toothpicks through their sails and then into the bases.

• TELESCOPES — Using markers, have the children color paper towel rolls. Next punch two holes at one end of each of their rolls and then loop pieces of yarn through the holes so the children can hang them around their necks. They can wear and use their telescopes all day.

• SAILOR CAPS — Let the children decorate white paper plates by gluing white styrofoam pieces on the top. Punch holes on each side and add yarn strings. Tie them on each sailor. (Can use for special party time activity.)

Cooking
GLOBE POPCORN BALLS

You'll Need:

1/4 cup margarine
   or butter
4 cups mini marshmallows
1/4 cup peanut butter
   (optional)
7 cups popped corn

To Make: Melt margarine over low heat in large pan. Add marshmallows and stir until melted. Add peanut butter. Pour over popcorn. Stir until well coated. Form into balls (grease hands or put plastic bags on hands to form balls). Makes 10 large or 15 medium balls.

Blocks

• SAILING — Convert your area into the Atlantic Ocean. Get a large box such as one from an appliance store. Cut it into the shape of a ship. Add sails to the ship by attaching dowel rods to the side of the box and gluing paper or cloth sails to them. Hoist a Spanish flag. Write Santa Maria on the side of the ship. Add paper towel roll telescopes, oars, empty food boxes, sailor caps, etc. If you have any type of model fish, scatter them around the ship.

Discovery

• SINK OR FLOAT — Have a tub of water and a container of objects which sink or float. You'll also need to make a "Sink or Float Board." Get a piece of posterboard. Draw a line down the middle. Write "SINK" at the top of one side and "FLOAT" at the top of the other.

To play have the children put one object in the water, decide if it sinks or floats and then put it on the appropriate side of the board. Continue in this manner until all of the objects have been sorted.

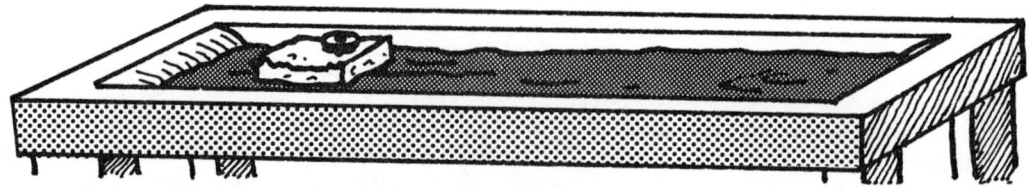

• BALANCE BOATS — Get a large tub of water, a styrofoam boat, and several different size metal washers. Encourage the children to put the washers in different areas of the boat. How can they arrange them to make the boat balance? How many large ones make the boat tip? How many small ones?

SNACK TIME

Snack

• Pass out a Globe Popcorn Ball to each child. Before eating, pretend the Popcorn Balls are globes. Have the children point to where Columbus might have begun his journey and then use their finger to travel across the ocean to the new land.

Now enjoy eating them with glasses of New World Grape Juice.

Place Settings

• Turn your snack area into the Santa Maria. Spread a sheet, bedspread, or blanket out on the floor. Put a Spanish flag in the middle of the 'ship'. Have the children wear their caps and sit around in the ship while they eat their snacks.

DISMISSAL TIME

Just before it is time to go home, hide small Spanish flags around the room. Have each child pretend he is Christopher Columbus, find a Spanish flag, and then search throughout the room for something new — such as a puzzle he hasn't tried yet, new cookie cutters in the art center, etc. When each child has found a new thing, he should tell you what it is and then get ready to leave.

HALLOWEEN PARTY

SPECIAL PARTY TIME

Several weeks before the party send a note home to the parents telling them that the children are going to have a parade at school to celebrate Halloween. Suggest that the costumes be very simple and that the children wear a minimal amount of make-up in place of masks. (An alternative to costumes would be for the children to make paper plate faces. They can do this by cutting out large holes for the eyes and then gluing a variety of collage materials to the plate. Attach a paint stir-stick for a handle.)

Have a parade around the school or your neighborhood as soon as the children arrive that day. They can show off the masks they made or their costumes. When you return have the children play the quiet game, *"Who's the Dog"*. (See activities below.) This will give them an opportunity to rest before taking off their costumes or putting their masks away.

Now play *"Bob For Apples"*. Put small apples in individual bowls of water. After each child has taken off his costume, he can bob for an apple. When he gets it, he can eat it.

CIRCLE TIME

Quiet Games

• WHO'S THE DOG — Describe one of the children's costumes or masks. The children guess who you're describing. When they have guessed who it is, that child stands. The children can add more facts about the costume or mask. Continue by describing the other children's costumes or masks.

• PUMPKIN PIE — Cut a large orange felt circle into eight to ten equal pieces. On each piece write a numeral or draw a specific number of dots.

   Pass out the pieces to the children. Call out *"I want a piece of pie with numeral 'one' written on it"* (or one dot). That child brings his piece of pie up and puts it on the felt board. Now call for piece of pie number *'two'*. Have that child put his piece next to the first one. Continue until the pie is finished.

• POSITIONAL PUMPKIN — Have a large plastic pumpkin and a small cat figurine.
   Place the pumpkin in the middle of your circle so that everyone can see it. Give the cat to a child. Say to him, *"Put your cat 'in' the pumpkin."* When he does, have him tap another child on the shoulder. That child picks up the cat and listens for the next direction such as, *"Put the cat 'under' the pumpkin"*. He does and taps another child. The game continues using other position words (over, next to, in the middle of, far away from, close to, etc.) until everyone has had at least one chance. Remember you can repeat position words.

23

Active Games

- ORANGE EATER — You'll need a large plastic jack-o-lantern with an open top.

  Show the children the jack-o-lantern. Tell them that he is very hungry and likes to eat orange objects. At a given signal, (such as a snap of your finger) they should quickly go around the classroom, find something orange to feed him, and bring it back to the circle. When everyone has returned let the children take turns feeding the jack-o-lantern. As they feed him, have the group call out the name of the object he's eating, such as *"an orange block"*.

- PIN THE NOSE ON THE PUMPKIN — Tape a large jack-o-lantern (without a nose) to the wall. Cut a black triangle for each child. Roll a piece of tape and fasten it to the back of each triangle.

  Have the children take turns putting a paper bag over their heads, walking to the jack-o-lantern, (hold their hands for guidance) and placing their triangles where they think the nose should be. As each child takes the bag off, talk about where he placed the triangle, rather than who placed their's the closest.

- MUSICAL PUMPKINS — Precut a construction paper pumpkin for each child. Spread all of the pumpkins (except one) in a circle on the floor. Have a special place near the game which the children can call a *'fence'*. (You might tie a piece of twine between two chairs.)

  Tell the children that you are going to play some Halloween music. As the music is playing they should walk around the pumpkins. When the music stops they should stand on a pumpkin close to them. One child will not be on a pumpkin. That child should take one of the pumpkins from the floor, and stand behind the fence. The music plays again, stops, the children move to a pumpkin, and one more child is added to the fence. While the *'pumpkins'* are standing behind the fence, pretend to turn each of them into a jack-o-lantern by using your index finger to draw the features. Continue until all of the pumpkins are behind the fence.

  EXTENSION: The children can use collage materials to convert their construction paper pumpkins into jack-o-lanterns.

- FIND THE FACE — Precut a construction paper pumpkin along with features for a jack-o-lantern face for each child.

Hide the facial features in the room. Give each child a pumpkin shape. When you say *"Decorate your pumpkin,"* the children should look for two eyes, a nose, and a mouth. After they've found them, they should bring them back to the group area and lay them on their pumpkin. Then they can help a friend who is still looking for all of his features.

When everyone has found his features, let the children glue them to their pumpkin shape.

Rhymes and Songs

LOOK WHO HAS COME TO SCHOOL TODAY
(tune: Mary Had a Little Lamb)

*Look who's come to school today,
School today, school today.
Look who's come to school today.
Today is Halloween.*

*A cowboy has come to school today,
School today, school today.
A cowboy has come to school today.
(Use costumes names or children's names
 as they hold their puppets up.)
Today is Halloween.*

A verse is sung for each child.

THE PUMPKIN'S HERE TODAY
(tune: Farmer In the Dell)

*The pumpkin's here today. The pumpkin's here today.
Hi, Ho it's Halloween, the pumpkin's here today.
The pumpkin takes a scarecrow, the pumpkin takes a scarecrow,
Hi, ho, it's Halloween, the pumpkin takes a scarecrow.*

(Use the names of other characters (costumes) the children have had on that day until all of the children are in the middle.)

ACTIVITY TIME

Art

• BLACK CATS — Precut black construction paper pieces which the children can roll into cone shapes for the cats' bodies. Have collage materials and glue available for them to use to decorate their cats.

Let the children roll their construction paper into cone shapes and glue or staple them closed. Have each child cut out a head shape. Using the collage materials and glue, the children can add facial features to the heads and then staple them to the bodies. Encourage them to add any additional features they would like such as tails, ears, etc.

Cooking

JACK-O-LANTERN FACES

You'll Need:

English muffins
Cheese slices
Olive pieces

To Make: Cut the cheese slices into rounds. Lay them on the English muffins. Let the children decorate each one with olive pieces. Toast them in the oven.

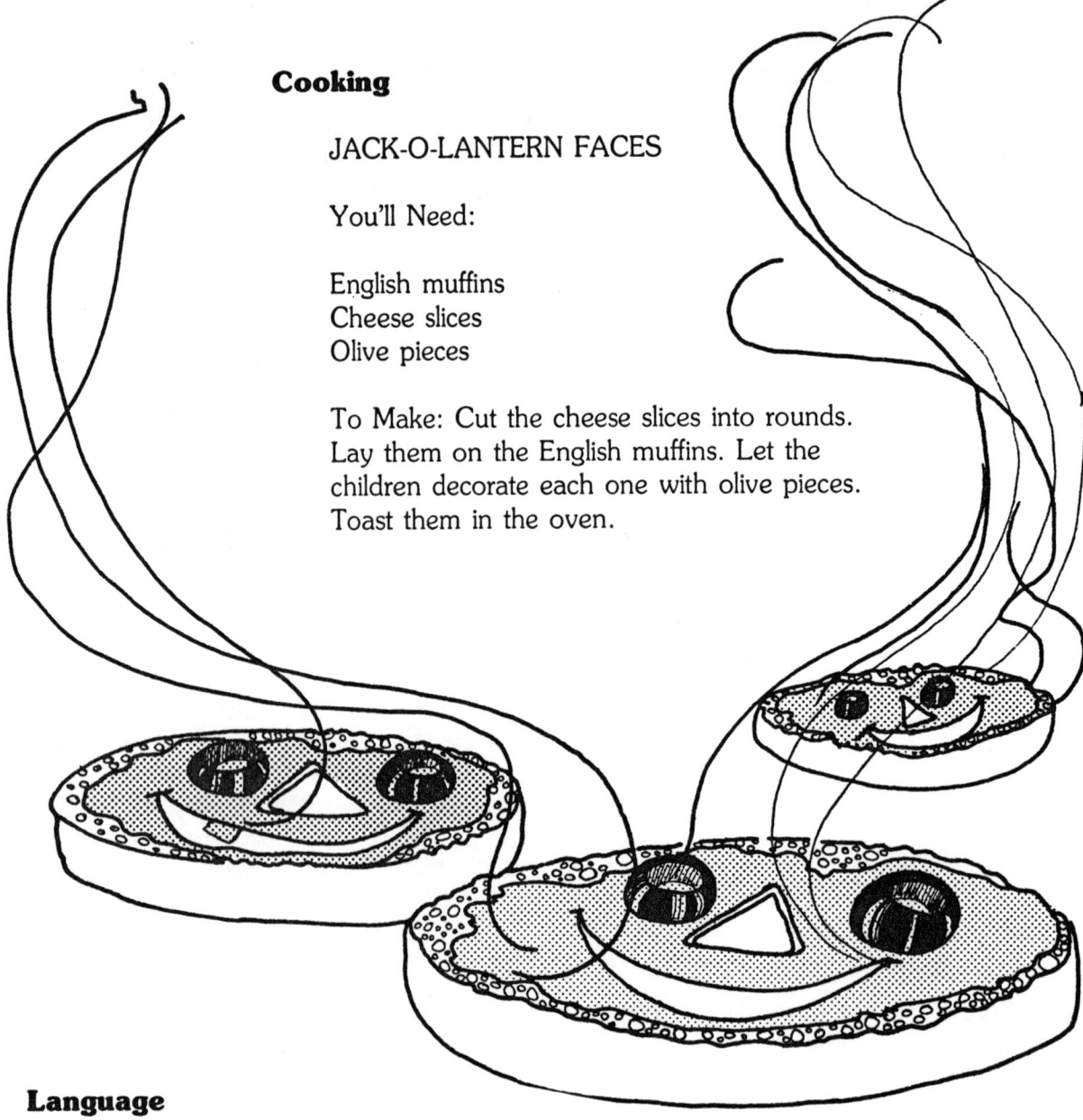

Language

• FELT BOARD PUMPKIN — Cut a large pumpkin out of orange felt and a variety of facial features out of black felt.

Put the felt board and pieces in the language center. Encourage the children to make jack-o-lantern faces. As they are mixing and matching the pieces talk to them about how their jack-o-lantern is feeling — happy, sad, silly, etc.

Discovery

• SPIDER COLLECTION — Have a spider or bug collection on the Discovery Table. Add a magnifying glass so the children can examine the collection more carefully. Talk about how many legs they can see, the colors, and so on.

Set books, posters, and magazines about bugs in the area. Sit with the children and talk about the pictures. Discuss and compare the different features. Which bugs do the children like best? Which one is the ugliest?

• GHOST WRITING — Have a bowl of lemon juice or milk, white paper, cotton swabs, and an overhead, slide or filmstrip projector. The children should dip cotton swabs into the liquid and draw designs on their paper. Redip whenever they want. When they've finished with the designs, they should let them dry, and then hold them up to the projector's light to see the results. Add more design if they'd like, let it dry, and look again.

Small Muscle

• DROP THE CLOTHESPINS IN THE JACK-O-LANTERN — Use a real or plastic Jack-O-Lantern. Have the children kneel on a chair and bend over the back to drop clothespins into the opening. When each child is finished, he should remove the clothespins and set them on the chair for another child.

SNACK TIME

Snack

• Enjoy the Jack-O-Lantern Treats with glasses of orange juice.

Table Decorations

• Have the children bring the cats they created at art to snack and place them in a line down the center of the table. They can talk about them while eating their jack-o-lanterns.

• Make nutcup treats for the children to take home. Fill small heavy-duty muffin cups with nuts and raisins. Add a pipe cleaner handle to each one. Put them by the children's places. Let the children know that they are going to take the nutcups home. After snack wrap each one in a napkin and have the children put them near their coats.

Place Settings

• The children use the jack-o-lanterns they made during the *'Find the Face'* game for placemats. (If you're not going to play this game have the children decorate pumpkins in the art area during activity time.)

• Have the children add Halloween stickers to their napkins.

• Make a special straw for each child by cutting small paper pumpkins and inserting straws through them.

DISMISSAL TIME

Name the costume that each child wore. Ask him how his character might move if he were going home. When he answers say,

— *"Cat Josuha is going to crawl home. Good-bye Cat."*

— *"Astronaut Luke will fly into outer space. Good-bye Astronaut."*

— *"Doctor Anne will ride to the hospital in an ambulance. Good-bye Doctor."*

Continue in this manner.

THANKSGIVING PARTY

SPECIAL PARTY TIME

To help the children better understand what happened at Plymouth Rock, act out the First Thanksgiving. First enjoy several rhymes and fingerplays. Now that the children are in the Thanksgiving mood, begin telling them about the First Thanksgiving. As you tell the story have the children pretend that they are Pilgrims and Indians. You might begin by having the children row their ship, the Mayflower, toward Plymouth Rock. Continue by having them cut trees for their homes, meet the Indians, plant corn, shoot wild game, etc. Because the pilgrims were thankful to be free in a new land they decided to have a big feast. They invited their friends the Indians to celebrate with them.

After the story go around the circle and let each child tell the others one thing for which he is thankful.

CIRCLE TIME

Quiet Games

• FEATHERS FOR FRAN — Cut feather shapes and matching six inch squares from many different kinds of wallpaper samples. Glue a sandpaper piece on the back of each feather. Make a turkey body and head from plain colored felt. Place the turkey on the feltboard. Say to the children, *"See our poor turkey Fran. She is so plain and has no feathers. I'm sure she is sad. Let's make her happy by giving her some colorful feathers."* Hold up a square of wallpaper. Say, *"Whoever has the feather that matches this pattern, put your feather on Fran."* Continue until all feathers are on Fran.

• TODAY OR LONG AGO — Before you play this game collect pictures of things the Pilgrims might have used and ones we use today, such as a horse, pump, ice, open fire, long dress, fireplace, car, plane, kitchen sink, bathtub, refrigerator, microwave oven, radio, TV, etc. Hold up two modern pictures and one Pilgrim picture. Ask your children to choose the thing which Pilgrims used. Continue until all of the pictures have been discussed.

• DISCUSS FEATHERS — Bring different types of feathers and objects in which feathers are used to show the children. For example you could have a feather duster, fishing lure (without hook), earrings, necklace, hairclips, hats, a small pillow, etc. Also provide pictures of birds such as peacock, eagle, duck or goose, and small bird. Talk about the different types of feathers. Tell the children you're going to put them on the Discovery Table.

Active Games

• TURKEY, TURKEY, WHERE ARE YOUR FEATHERS? — The children stand in a circle. Pick a child to begin. This child struts around the circle, stopping at a friend to ask, *"Turkey, turkey, where are your feathers?"* The child responds, *"I don't know but I'll go see."* The child fans his hands out behind him and struts to another child, asking the same question. This continues until everyone has had a turn. The last child struts to the teacher who answers, *"Here they are"* as she pulls out craft feathers and gives one to each child. Talk about the colors of each feather.

• PIN THE WADDLE ON THE TURKEY — Tape a large paper turkey on the wall. Cut out red waddles for each child. Roll a piece of tape and fasten it to the back of each waddle.
   Have the children take turns putting a paper bag over their heads, walking to the turkey, (hold their hands for safety) and attempting to put the waddle under the turkey's chin. When the child takes his bag off, talk with him about where he placed the waddle — close to or far away from the turkey's chin.

Rhymes and Songs

THIS IS THE WAY THE PILGRIMS CAME
(tune: Here We Go 'Round the Mulberry Bush)

This is the way the pilgrims came, the pilgrims came, the pilgrims came,
This is the way the pilgrims came,
On that first Thanksgiving Day. (Children march around the circle as they sing.)

This is the way they built their homes, (Hammer while singing)

This is the way the Indian hunted, (Shoot a bow and arrow while singing)

This is the way they planted corn, (Plant while singing)

This is the way they cooked their food, (Stir food while singing)

This is the way they all gave thanks, (Bow head while singing)

This is the way they ate their feast, (Eat while singing)

THANKSGIVING DINNER
(tune: Frere Jacque)

We eat turkey, we eat turkey
Oh so good. Oh so good.
Always on Thanksgiving
Always on Thanksgiving
Yum, yum, yum. Yum, yum, yum.

THREE FAT TURKEYS
(tune: Three Blind Mice)

Three fat turkeys, three fat turkeys
See how they strut, see how they strut
They spread their tails in a fan to say
We won't be here on Thanksgiving Day
We're sure to run the other way
Three fat turkeys, three fat turkeys.
                    by Susan Spaete

Story

• During the week prior to Thanksgiving, send home a sheet of construction paper with each child and have him and his family write a sentence about why they are thankful. The child can use crayons or markers to illustrate the paper in any way he chooses. He should bring this back on or before the party day. Punch all of the pages and loosely tie them together with yarn to form a book. Read this book for your Thanksgiving story.

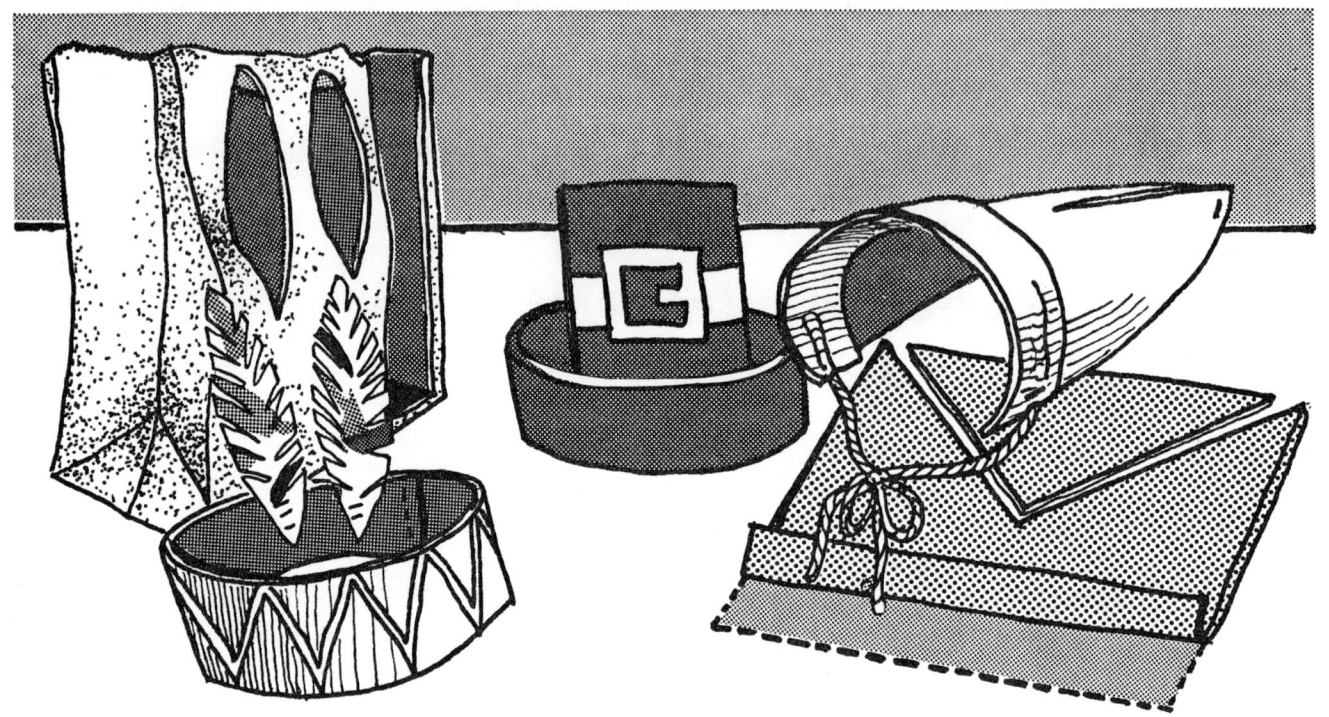

ACTIVITY TIME

Art

• THANKSGIVING HEADBANDS — Let the children choose whether they would like to make Indian headbands or Pilgrim hats.

— Indian Headbands: Using grocery bags, cut two inch bands in lengths to fit children's heads. Use the remaining paper from the bag to cut feather shapes. Have the children color and fringe them and then staple them to the band.

— Pilgrim Hats: Cut a two inch band out of black paper to fit each child's head. Let the children cut a black hat shape and yellow buckle. Glue it to the hat. Staple the hat to the band and staple the band to fit.

— Pilgrim Bonnets: Using a 24" x 24" piece of paper, fold the bottom edge up about one inch. The other edge is cut from the top corners to the center. These edges are overlapped and stapled to fit each child's head. Strings may be attached for support.

• WE GIVE THANKS PLACEMATS — Have the children look through magazines, cut out the things they are thankful for, and glue them all over a 9" x 12" piece of construction paper. On the top they can glue the title *"We Give Thanks"* which has been prepared and cut out ahead of time. The mat may be covered with clear contact.

Cooking — The children can prepare all or part of a Thanksgiving Feast to enjoy together. They should begin the food preparation as soon as they come to school. (You might want to let them prepare several of the foods the day before.)

CORNBREAD

You'll Need:

1 cup cornmeal
1 cup flour
4 t baking powder
2 T brown sugar
1/2 cup powdered milk
2 beaten eggs
1 cup milk
1/4 cup shortening

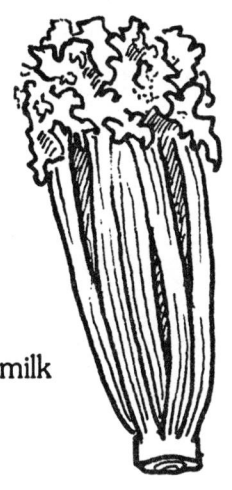

To Make: Combine ingredients and mix well. Pour into well oiled pan. Bake at 400° for 10-15 minutes. This will serve 16 if made in corn irons. It may be made in an 8" × 10" pan. It may be doubled or make two batches.

FRESH VEGETABLES

You'll Need:

Carrots
Celery
Broccoli
Cauliflower
Cucumber
Green pepper

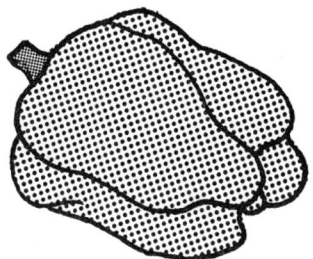

To Make: Wash a variety of vegetables. Cut them into serving pieces. Put them on a vegetable plate.

PILGRIM STEW

You'll Need:

6 cups of water
Beef bone
1 onion
1-2 celery stalks
1-2 carrots
Tomatoes, canned or fresh
1-2 potatoes
Corn, canned or fresh
Any other vegetables the children would like

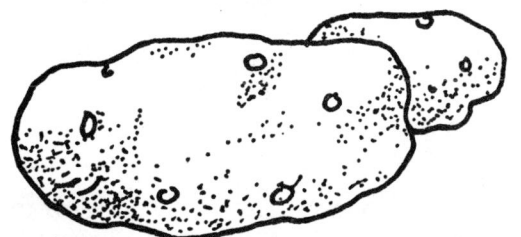

To Make: Ahead of time simmer the bone with the water to make broth. The children should wash, peel, and cut the vegetables into small pieces. (If an adult cuts them into sticks first, it is easier for the children to cut.) Add these and any other ingredients to the broth and simmer for about 45 minutes.

YOGURT DIP

You'll Need:

1 cup yogurt
1 cup mayonnaise
1 T lemon juice
1 T fresh parsley

To Make: Mix all of the ingredients and refrigerate.

SNACK TIME

Snack

• Have a Thanksgiving feast by serving the Pilgrim stew, cornbread, vegetables, and milk or for a lighter snack, have fresh vegetables with the yogurt dip.

Table Decorations

• Have a display of dried fruits and fresh vegetables in the middle of the table. Name the fruits and vegetables as you eat.

Place Settings

• Have the children bring their *"We Give Thanks"* placemats to the table when they have finished making them at art. Let each child use his for the Feast.

• While the children are waiting have them make Apple Turkeys to take home. At each place put an apple, four toothpicks, a raisin, and a handful of Cheerios®. Have the children form the turkey by putting the raisin onto one toothpick and then poking it into the apple for the head. Poke the other three toothpicks into the apple for a tail and add all of the Cheerios®.

• Have napkins and tableware.

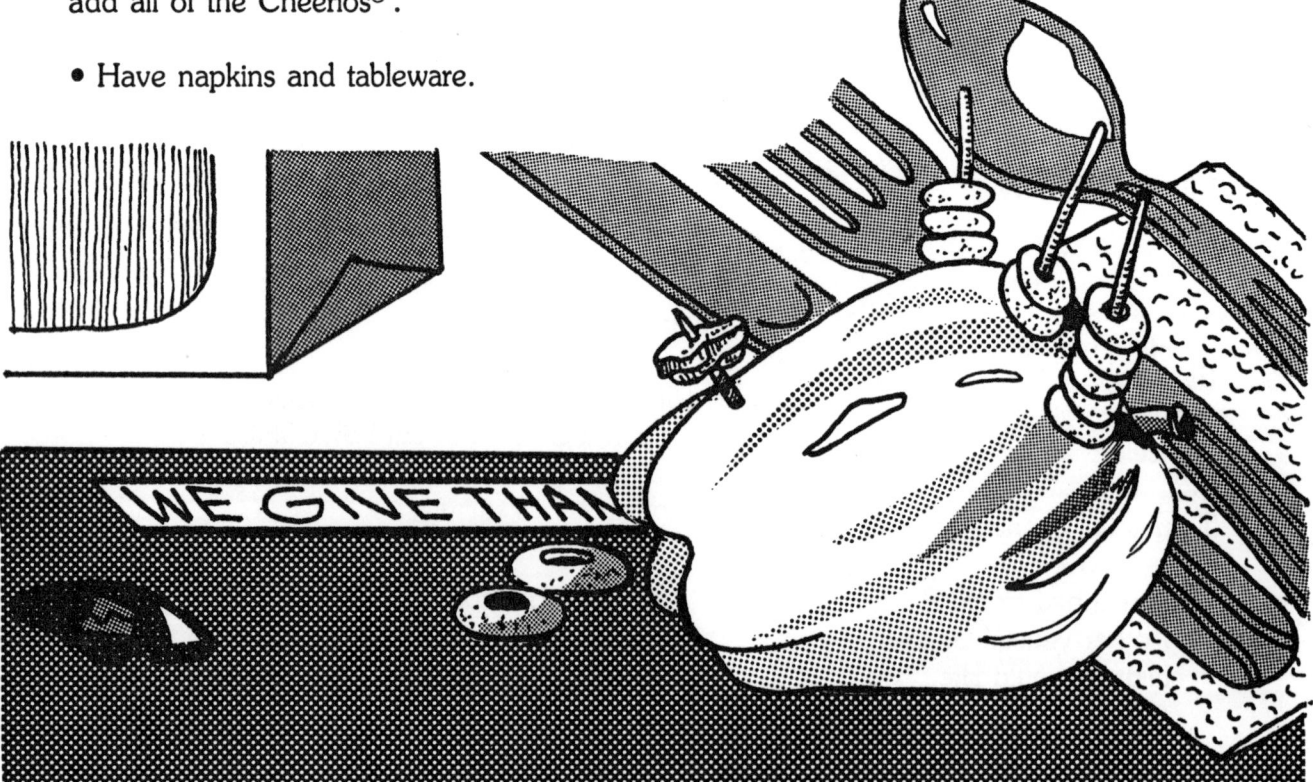

DISMISSAL TIME

Talk with the children about what they are going to do over Thanksgiving. Are they visiting someone? Who? What are they going to eat? Remind them that they come back to school after the weekend and tell them you are looking forward to seeing them again. Happy Thanksgiving!

HANUKKAH PARTY

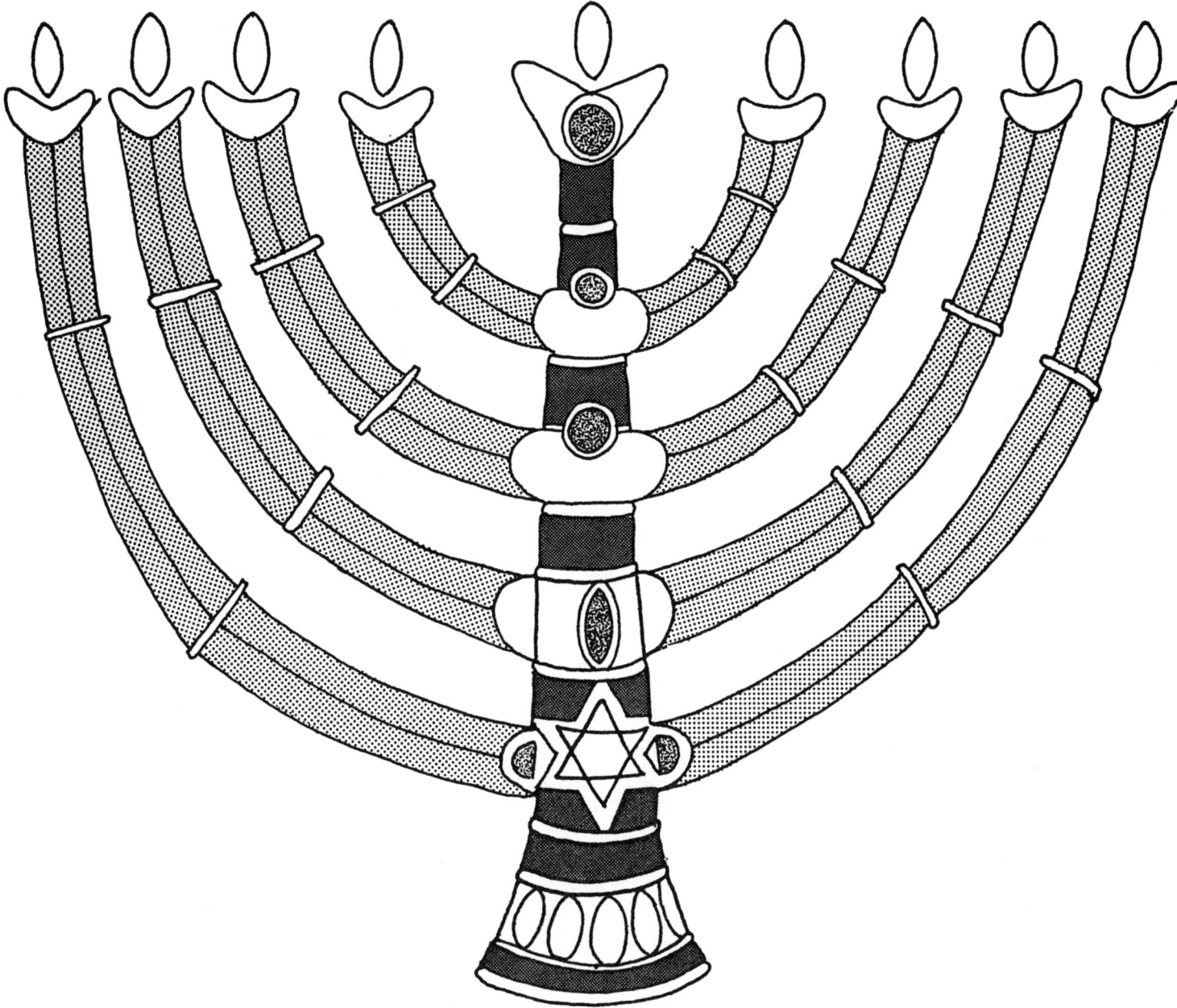

SPECIAL PARTY TIME

Invite a special guest to tell the children the story of Hanukkah. After the guest has finished, play a game called 'Candle Match'. You'll need to cut pairs of construction paper candles all the same size and color. Add different colored flames to each pair of candles.

To play, randomly pass out the pairs of candles giving each child one candle. Have each child look at the color of his flame. On a given signal the child should hold up his candle and look for the other child holding the candle flame that matches his. When the partners find each other they should stand together. When all of the pairs are together, have the partners hold up their candles and call out the color of their flames.

CIRCLE TIME

Quiet Games

• COLORED CANDLES — Make two felt menorahs, one blue and one white. Cut blue and white felt candles for each one.

Put the two menorahs on the felt board. Pass out the candles to the children. Point to one of the menorahs. The children holding the matching color candles should hold them up. Call on one child to put his candle in the menorah. Point to one of the menorahs again and continue playing until both menorahs have all of their candles.

• WHICH COMES FIRST? — Using posterboard, cut eight graduated candles in holders.

Lay the candles in order on the floor. Have a child come and point to the largest one, then the smallest one. Now have all of the children cover their eyes. Mix up the order of the candles. Have the children uncover their eyes and put the candles back in order beginning with the largest one. Repeat, only this time begin the order with the smallest one.

Active Games

- DREIDEL PLAY — Make a simple dreidel by covering a small milk carton with construction paper. Write the numbers 1, 2, 3, or 4 on the sides of the dreidel. Put an unsharpened pencil through the middle of the carton.

Each child will get a turn to spin the dreidel and lead the group in an exercise of his choice. Whatever number is up when the dreidel stops spinning indicates how many times the group should do the exercise. For example, if the dreidel lands with a '2' showing, the children will do two 'arm swings'.

Rhymes and Songs

THE FESTIVAL OF LIGHTS
(tune: Mary Had a Little Lamb)

*Blue and white for Hanukkah, Hanukkah, Hanukkah,
Blue and white for Hanukkah,
The Festival of Lights.*

*We give gifts at Hanukkah, Hanukkah, Hanukkah
We give gifts at Hanukkah,
The Festival of Lights.*

*Light the candles at Hanukkah, Hanukkah, Hanukkah
Light the candles at Hanukkah,
The Festival of Lights.*

Story — Enjoy using THE PICTURE BOOK OF HANUKKAH by David A. Adler to tell the children the story of Hanukkah. You might read the book HANUKKAH IN MY HOUSE by Norma Simon.

ACTIVITY TIME

Art

• SOFT DOUGH — Using your favorite recipe make a fresh batch of soft dough. Have small candles in a margarine tub. Encourage the children to make menorahs by forming the dough and adding the candles.

• GLITTERING CANDLES — Precut a large construction paper candle shape for each child. Have him brush glue on his candle and sprinkle glitter on it. Let it dry and then gently shake off the excess glitter.

• HANUKKAH PLACEMATS — Give each child a blue piece of construction paper. Let him use white crayon to draw any design on it he'd like.

Blocks

• HIDING IN THE DARK — Set a large appliance box or tent in the area. Tack aluminum foil Stars of David inside the box or the tent. Have several flashlights for the children to use to reflect the light while in the dark.

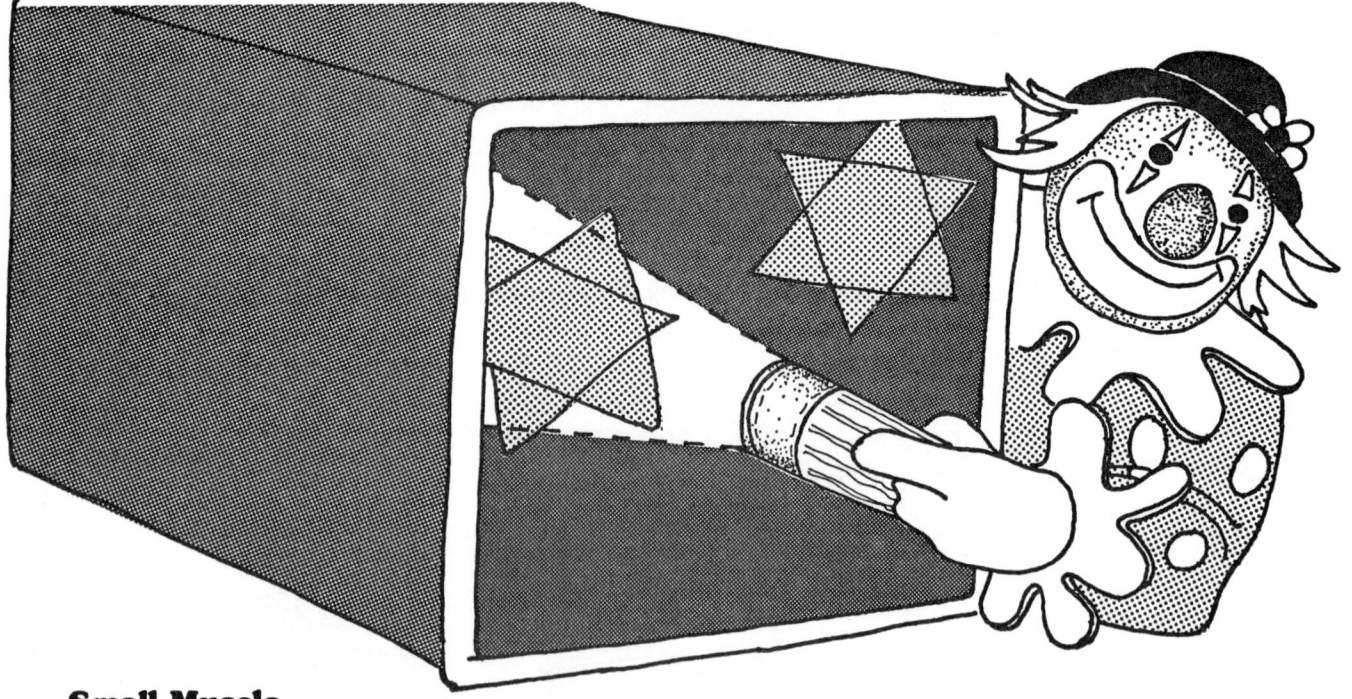

Small Muscle

• NAPKIN ROLLS — Have a stack of paper napkins. Have the children roll the napkins into candle shapes, tape them closed, and carry them over to the snack area so they'll be ready for snack time.

• CANDLE HOLDERS — Using construction paper, cut candles of several different widths and holders whose openings match the widths of the different candles. Glue the holders to a piece of posterboard. Put the candles in a small box. Have the children match the candles to their appropriate holders. (If this is too difficult use colors that match.)

Cooking

POTATO LATKES

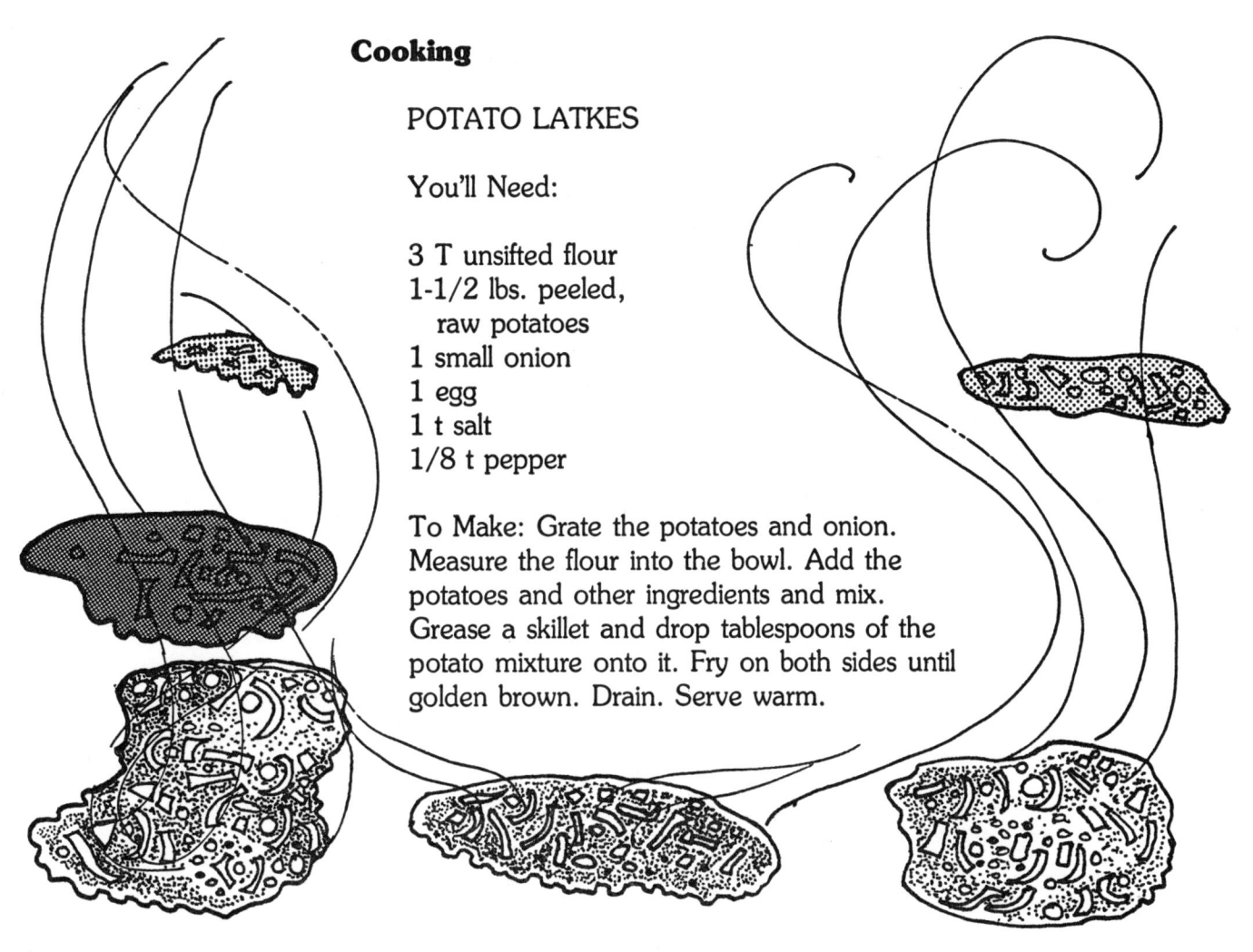

You'll Need:

3 T unsifted flour
1-1/2 lbs. peeled, raw potatoes
1 small onion
1 egg
1 t salt
1/8 t pepper

To Make: Grate the potatoes and onion. Measure the flour into the bowl. Add the potatoes and other ingredients and mix. Grease a skillet and drop tablespoons of the potato mixture onto it. Fry on both sides until golden brown. Drain. Serve warm.

SNACK TIME

Snack

- Serve the potato latkes along with applesauce and sour cream. Enjoy with glasses of milk.

Table Decoration

- Put a real menorah in the middle of the table along with the dough menorahs which the children made.

Place Settings

- The children can use the blue placemats which they decorated with white crayons and the napkins they rolled up like candles.

- Add tableware.

DISMISSAL TIME

During a time when the children are not present, hide chocolate gelt, play coins, or a treat wrapped in aluminum foil around the room. Just before it is time to go home tell them that there is a treat hidden around the room for each of them. When you say, "Go" they can begin looking. After each child finds his treat he should get ready to go.

CHRISTMAS PARTY

SPECIAL PARTY TIME

Arrange ahead of time for Santa Claus or a group of carolers to visit the school. When Santa arrives let those children who would like to talk with him do so. Sing several songs and then have Santa or the carolers distribute small gifts to each child. When all of the children have received their gifts, count to three and let them open their presents. (This is also an appropriate time to distribute gifts the teacher is giving to the children if this is customary in your school.)

CIRCLE TIME

Quiet Games

- COUNTDOWN CALENDAR — On December 1st make red and green chains with twenty-five loops each. (If December 1st doesn't fall on a school day, adjust the number accordingly.) Hang one chain in the classroom and let each of the children take one home. Every day have a child pull a loop off of the chain. Encourage the children to do the same activity at home. On the day of the Christmas party, be sure to distinguish between the party and Christmas Day. Remind the children that it is not Christmas until all of the loops are off of the chain.

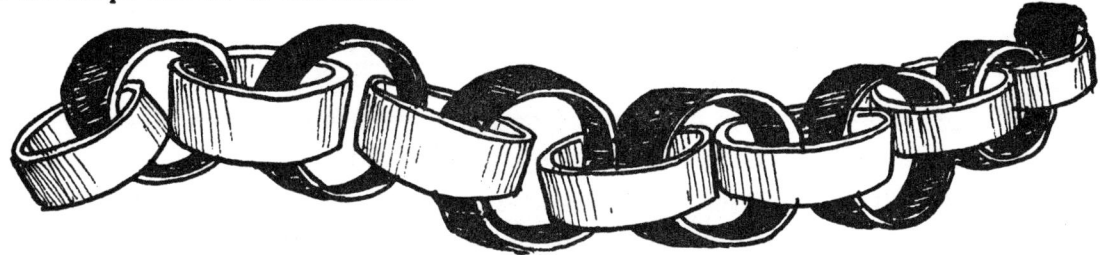

- STOCKING FUN — Precut construction paper stockings for the children. Write each child's name on a stocking.
  Bring the stockings to show the children. Hold each one up and have the children identify their names and the color of their stockings.
  Extension: The children can take their stockings to the art area, drizzle glue along the letters, and shake glitter on them. Let the stockings dry and then carefully shake the excess glitter off of them.

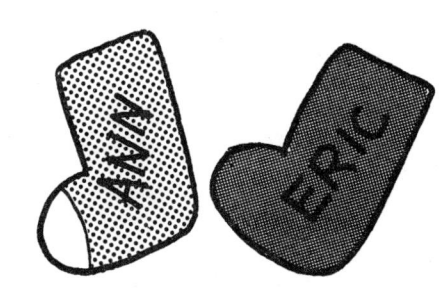

- CHRISTMAS BOX — Wrap a large box like a gift, being certain that you can lift the top off. Cut a hole in one side of the box large enough for a child to stick his arm through. Fill the box with a variety of Christmas items, such as a cookie cutter, a miniature reindeer, a stocking, a candy cane, a Santa statue, etc.
  Before playing, show the children all of the items. Talk about each one. Then put all of the objects into the box. Have a child come up, put his hand into the box, and grab an object but not take it out. He should feel the object and guess what it is. Carefully lift the box top and take out the item he is holding. Everyone can name the object together.

• **STRING OF LIGHTS** — Cut three felt Christmas tree lights out of each of the eight basic colors. For example, three red, three blue, three yellow, and so on.

Drape a piece of yarn across your felt board. Make a pattern of lights on your yarn such as red, green, red, green, red, _____. Point to each light and have the children call out the color. When you get to the end ask them what color they think comes next. Have a child come up, find a green light, and add it to the pattern. Read the pattern again and then remove the lights. Now have the children cover their eyes and put up another pattern. When they uncover their eyes, they should read the pattern and figure out which light would come next. Continue with five or six more patterns.

Active Games

• **CHRISTMAS EVE** — Divide the group of children in half. One group is sleeping children, the other group is Santa and his elves. Have the first group lie down and pretend to sleep. Santa and his elves quietly tiptoe towards the children. The teacher shouts, *"Santa is here!"* With that the sleeping children get up and chase Santa and the elves. When a child is caught he becomes sleepy. Now Santa and the elves sleep and the children creep up toward the North Pole. The teacher shouts, *"The children are coming!"* Santa and the elves try to catch the children as they run home. Play several times. You may want to switch roles.

• **HIDE THE ORNAMENT** — Choose a small group of children to leave the room. Hide an ornament in the room. When the children return they must find the ornament by listening as the others clap. Soft clapping indicates the searchers are getting further from the ornament and louder clapping signals the group is getting closer to it.

• **ELF, ELF, SANTA** — The children sit in a circle. A child is chosen to be 'It'. He walks around the circle touching each child as he goes, saying, *"Elf, Elf . . . Santa"*. The 'Santa' child gets up and chases the 'It' child back to Santa's place. Santa becomes 'It' and the game continues.

Rhymes and Songs

HERE WE GO 'ROUND THE CHRISTMAS TREE
(tune: Here We Go 'Round the Mulberry Bush)

Here we go 'round the Christmas tree, the Christmas tree, the Christmas tree.
Here we go 'round the Christmas tree, for Christmas time is here.

This is the way we put up the tree,

This is the way we hang up the lights.

Continue with the children's decorating suggestions. End with the ornament you put on the top.

Story

- Read or sing T'WAS THE NIGHT BEFORE CHRISTMAS by Clement Clarke Moore, illustrated by Gyo Fujikawa or ON CHRISTMAS EVE and CHRISTMAS IN THE BARN by Margaret Wise Brown.

ACTIVITY TIME

Art

- STAR — Cut a large piece of styrofoam into one inch cubes. Have the children poke rounded toothpicks into all sides of the cubes. Let the children paint the toothpicks and cubes yellow and then sprinkle them while wet with silver or gold glitter. Add a string to each star by poking a threaded needle through the cube and tying it off.

Cooking

REINDEER SANDWICHES

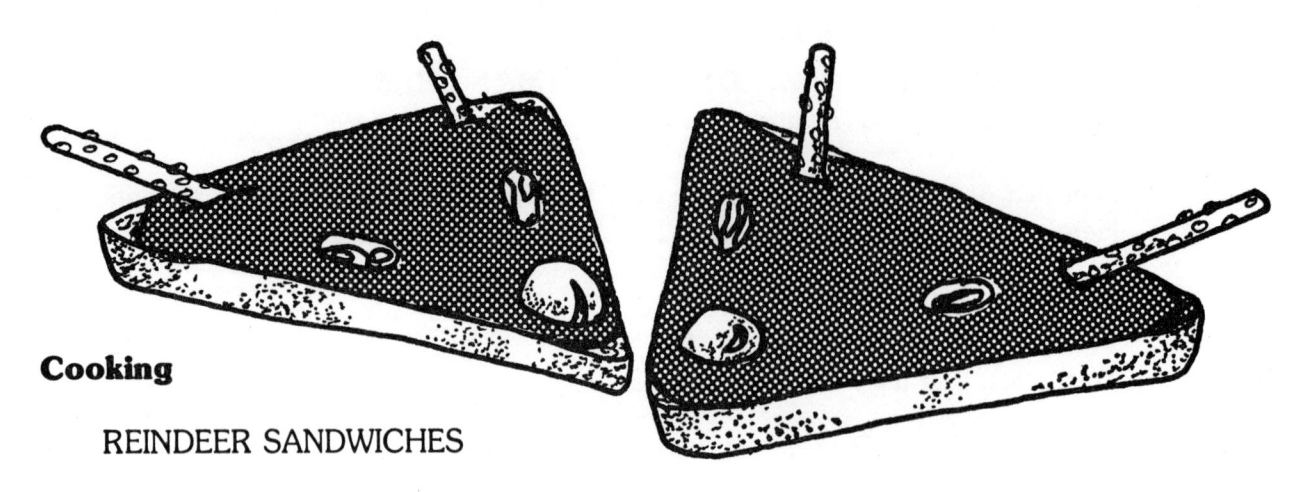

You'll Need:

Bread
Peanut Butter
Pretzels
Raisins
Cherries

To Make: Spread the peanut butter on the bread. Cut the bread diagonally in half. Add pretzels for the antlers, raisins for the eyes, and a half of cherry for the nose.

Blocks

• DOWN THE CHIMNEY — Encourage the children to use the blocks to build a chimney for Santa. You might want to include some reindeer, a sleigh, and a small Santa doll who can go down the chimney when it is built.

Dramatic Play

• NORTH POLE — Put a variety of Santa Claus props in the area. You might include Santa and elf costumes, wrapped gifts, a bag, toys, and stockings.

Discovery

• EVERGREEN BOUGHS — Have a display of different boughs and greens from a variety of evergreen trees and bushes. Compare the length of the needles, smells, colors, textures, and so on. You might add a magnifying glass for closer examination.

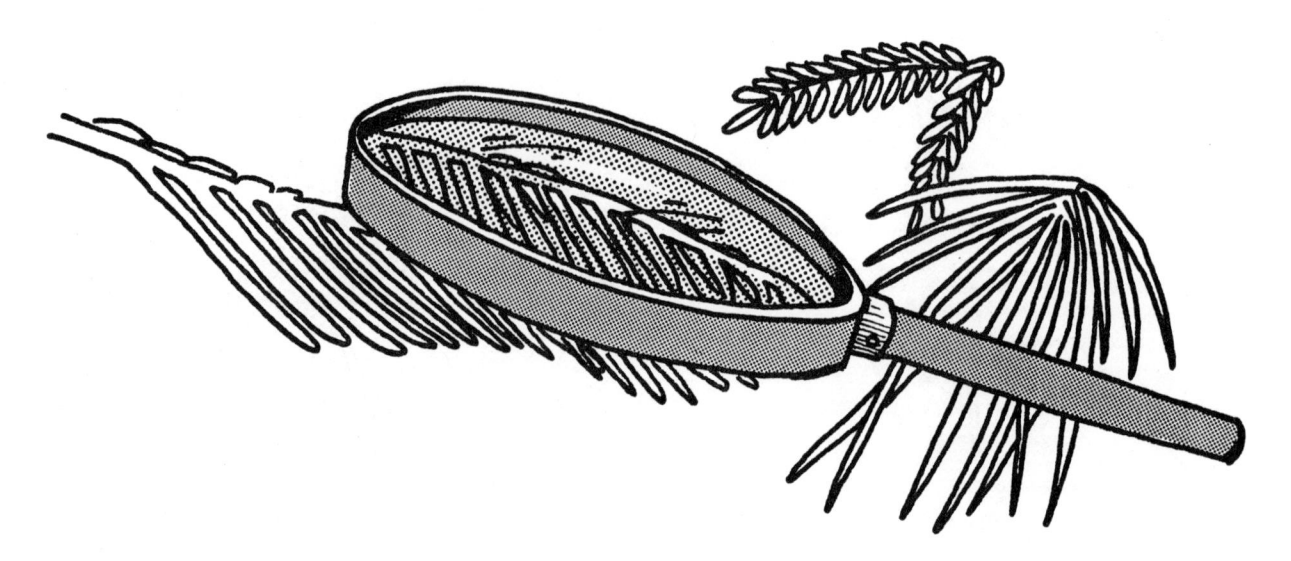

Small Muscle

• WRAPPING PAPER MATCH — To make the game you'll need a piece of posterboard and a variety of wrapping papers. Cut each type of wrapping paper into two identical squares about 3"×3". Using rubber cement or watered down white glue mount one of each pattern on the posterboard. Cover the mates with clear Contact® and put them in an envelope or small box.

To play have a child pull out one of the squares, find its matching square on the posterboard, and lay it on top. Continue until all of the wrapping paper squares have been matched.

Language

• OUR CHRISTMAS TREE — Have four separate pictures showing the steps of decorating a tree: 1. Buying a tree, 2. Taking it home, 3. Decorating it, and 4. Putting the final ornament on top. The children should lay the pictures on the floor, look at them, and put them in the correct order. Talk about the sequence with the children.

• DECORATE THE FELT TREE — Cut out a large felt Christmas tree along with a variety of felt ornaments. Encourage the children to have fun decorating and re-decorating their tree.

SNACK TIME

Snack

• Enjoy Reindeer Sandwiches with glasses of Christmas punch or milk.

Table Decorations

• Have a display of different Christmas tree ornaments down the middle of the table. Talk with the children about what types of ornaments they use to decorate their trees. Are any of them similar to the ones on the table?

Place Settings

• Use red and green pieces of construction paper for placemats.

• Have the children put the glittering stars they made during activity time at their places.

• Place a napkin and small candy cane at each child's place.

DISMISSAL TIME

Return to the Countdown Calendar (see Quiet Games). Count with the children how many days are left until Christmas. Remind them when they will return to school. Sing at least one Christmas carol and then help each child gather up all of his materials.

MARTIN LUTHER KING, JR. DAY

SPECIAL PARTY TIME

Martin Luther King Jr. believed in solving problems peacefully. Ask the children what they think this means. Relating specific incidences, ask them how they can solve problems peacefully at school, home, and play.

After discussing peace, tell the children that certain signs and symbols mean peace. Have two children come up to the front. (Tell the others to watch what these two children are going to do.) Whisper to them to shake hands. After shaking hands discuss what the children did and what it meant. Now have two other children come up. Whisper to them to give each other a hug. Have the others watch and then discuss what happened. Have pictures of other symbols which show peace such as a dove with an olive branch, a circle and a white flag. Discuss these also.

After discussing the meanings of the pictures and signs tell the children that you are going to say a *"peace word"*. When you say the word they should do an action which represents that word such as when you say *"dove"*, you want them to flap their arms like a bird, when you say *shake hands"*, they should turn to their neighbors and shake hands, and so on.

CIRCLE TIME

Quiet Games

• GUEST SPEAKER — A few weeks before the party contact a guest who could come and talk with the children about how Martin Luther King made the world a better place. Remind your speaker the talk should be informal and about 5-10 minutes long.

On the day of the party introduce your guest. After your guest has finished speaking invite him/her to stay for the remainder of the party.

• PEACE CIRCLE — Have all of the children cross their arms in front of their bodies and then hold their neighbor's hands. While they are all in this circle have them look at each other and say, *"Peace"*. Then tell them that they should all count to three. When they say, *"three"* they should squeeze each other's hands in a *"peace squeeze"*.

• WHAT SHOULD YOU DO? — Say to the children, *"We know that Martin Luther King believed in solving problems peacefully, that is without fighting. If you do the same thing what would you do if . . .* (Discuss each of these and other circumstances.)

— *"You were playing with the blocks and someone came and knocked them down. Would you get angry and yell at the child or ask the child to help you rebuild them? What should the child who knocked them down do? Run away or come back, say he is sorry, and help rebuild them?"*

— *"If there is a new girl in class that is different from everyone else, what should you do? Pretend she isn't there or ask her to play?"*

— *"You are watching television with your sister. She wants to watch one show and you want another. What should you do? Fight about it or talk it over?"*

Active Games

• OLIVE BRANCH — The children form a circle. One child is chosen to be the dove. The dove goes to the center and closes his eyes. The teacher quietly hands a twig or olive branch to a child who holds it behind his back. When a signal is given all the children say *"Peace"*. The dove opens his eyes and flies around to find the olive branch. When he finds it, he holds it until the new dove (child who had branch) goes to the center and closes his eyes. The old dove gives the branch to a new child. This is continued until everyone has had a turn.

Rhymes and Songs

HANDSHAKE

My hands can wave "Hi".
My hands can wave "Bye".
My hands can say other things too.
My hands can show that you are my friend and
That I really like you. (Give a handshake to a friend.)

by Susan Spaete

DR. KING
(tune: Bingo)

Dr. King was a man
And he had a dream
PEACE, PEACE, PEACE
And he dreamed of PEACE!

Dr. King was a man
And he had a dream
LOVE, LOVE, LOVE (hold 'V' two counts)
And he dreamed of LOVE!

by Susan Spaete

MARTIN LUTHER KING, JR.
(tune: Row, Row, Row Your Boat)

Martin, Martin Luther King,
Was a man of peace.
He said we should live as friends,
And let our fighting cease.

Martin, Martin Luther King,
Was a man of love.
He preached for equal rights to all,
And guidance from above.

Martin, Martin Luther King,
Was a man who dared.
To speak the things he truly thought,
And tell us that he cared.

by Dick Wilmes

Story

• Read MARTIN LUTHER KING DAY by Linda Lowery and THE BUTTER BATTLE BOOK by Dr. Seuss to the children.

ACTIVITY TIME

Art

• DOVE MOBILE — Have the children cut out a large, simple white bird from construction paper. Help them cut a slit in the center of each one. Give each child several pieces of white tissue cut in 4"×6" rectangles. Have him fold the tissue paper on the six inch side like a fan. Insert the tissue into the slot on bird. Tape a twig to the beak. Attach a string. The children can make two or three and hang them from a hanger.

• PEACE PLACEMATS — Have each child cut out a large circle from construction paper. Write *"PEACE"* on each one. Let the children use tempera paint and narrow brushes to paint over each of the letters. Let the placemats dry and put them near the snack table.

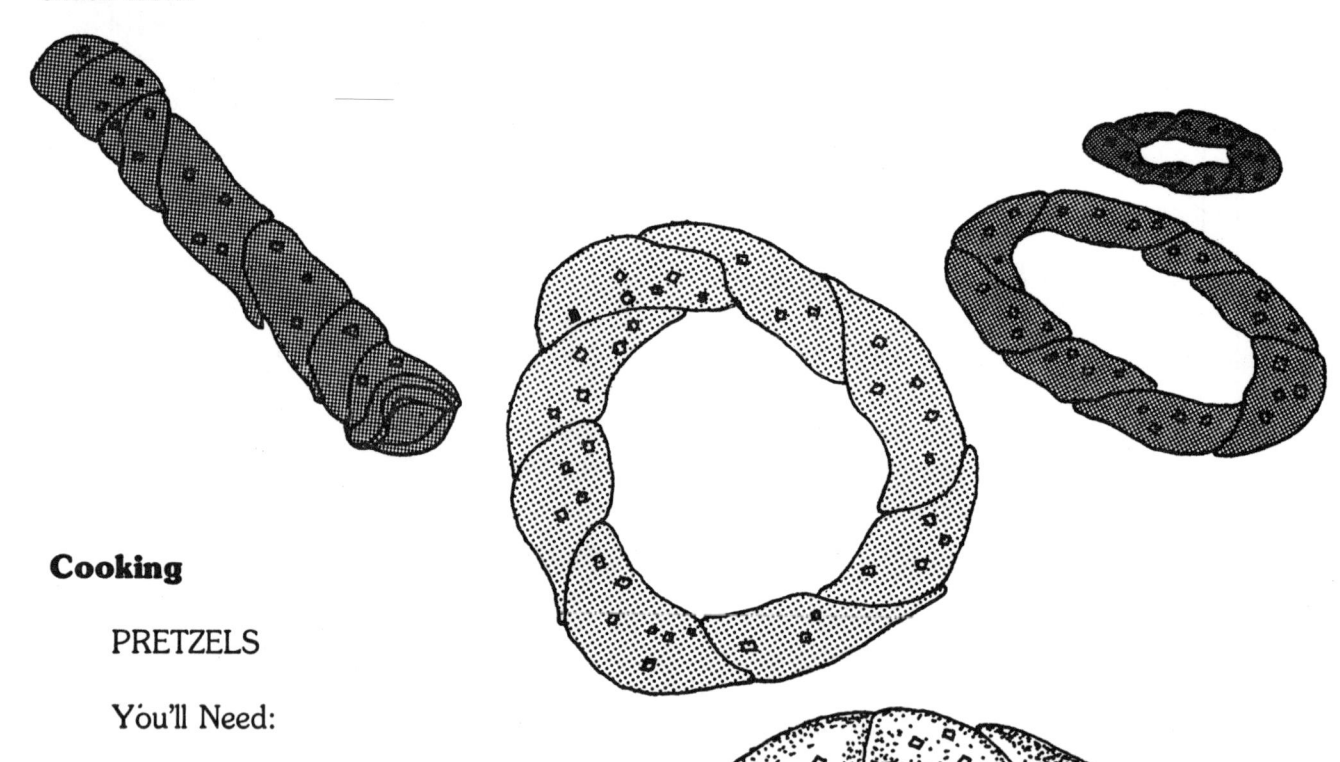

Cooking

PRETZELS

You'll Need:

1 pkg yeast
1-1/2 cups warm water
1/2 t sugar
4 cups flour, sifted
1 egg, beaten
coarse salt

To Make: In a large bowl dissolve the yeast in the water. Add the sugar. Let it rest for one hour. Blend in the flour and knead the dough on a floured surface until smooth. Let rise until doubled. Roll out the dough. Cut it into strips. Roll the strips into ropes and twist into peace circle shapes. Place on greased cookie sheet. Brush with egg and sprinkle with salt. Bake at 425° for 15 minutes. Serve warm. Makes thirty small pretzels,

Dramatic Play

• Convert the area into a restaurant. Use a tablecloth, pads of paper, menu with pictures, pencils, cash register, playdough, plastic foods, etc. Make a sign which reads *"EVERYONE IS WELCOME, PLEASE COME IN"*.

Language

• Children dictate into a tape recorder or to an adult what they would do to help keep Martin Luther King, Jr.'s dream of love, peace, and justice alive.

SNACK TIME

Snack

• Enjoy warm Pretzels and glasses of milk with the children and their Guest Speaker.

Place Settings

• Hang the Dove Mobiles over the table.

• Have the children use the Peace Placemats they made at art.

DISMISSAL TIME

In 1986 people in the United States celebrated Martin Luther King, Jr. Day for the first time. At that time, many children let helium balloons go up into the sky. Tell the children that they are going to do the same thing. (You may wish to send a note home a few days before the party inviting your parents to participate.)

Give each child a helium filled colored balloon to carry outdoors. Have everyone stand together and count to three. When they say *"three"* they should let their balloons float into the sky. Watch the many colors go up together.

GROUNDHOG'S DAY

SPECIAL PARTY TIME

Tell the children the legend of the groundhog seeing his shadow. Now have the children pretend they are groundhogs, take a walk, and see if the groundhogs can find their shadows.

The groundhog is an animal who lives in a burrow. Legend says that he is somewhat of a weather forecaster. On February 2nd he pokes his head out of his hole. If he sees his shadow, it frightens him and he ducks back into his hole and sleeps for six more weeks of winter. If he does not see his shadow, he feels safe and continues out of the hole. This means that spring is very close.

Now that the children know the legend, they're ready to be groundhogs. When everyone is outside have the children look for their shadows. If they find them they get frightened and curl up into a small ball. If they don't see them they can continue their walk around the neighborhood.

When you return to the classroom, discuss what type of weather, Spring or Winter, will follow.

CIRCLE TIME

Quiet Games

• DISCUSSING THE GROUNDHOG — Talk with the children about groundhogs. (Check out a poster of one from your library.) Tell the children that groundhogs are about the size of large squirrels. They live in holes in the ground called burrows. Ask the children what it would be like to live in a burrow. What would they do all day? Groundhogs are vegetarians. Discuss what they eat — nuts, berries, bark, and other things they find in the forest. Groundhogs hibernate in the winter, that is, they go into a deep sleep for the cold months. Do the children think they would like to sleep for the whole winter? What do the children do in the winter while the groundhog is hibernating?

Active Games

• FIND YOUR SHADOW — Before the game cut matching pairs of black and white shapes, numbers, letters, toys, and/or foods.

To play, give half of the children black cut-outs and the other half matching white cut-outs. When you say *"Find your shadow"* each child should look for the person holding his identical figure. When everyone is paired with his shadow, go around and have the children name the figures they are holding. Mix up the pairs or use different ones and play again.

• COME OUT GROUNDHOG — All but one of the children group together behind an arbitrary line. One child pretends to be a sleeping groundhog curled up about twenty feet away from the group.

To play, the children quietly creep up to the groundhog and ask, *"Groundhog, groundhog, will you come out today?"* If the groundhog answers, *"Yes, I will"*, he gets up and chases the children back to their goal. Anyone he catches becomes a groundhog with him. If he says, *"No, I won't"* the group keeps creeping closer and asks again until he says, *"Yes, I will."*

Rhymes and Songs

A GROUNDHOG
(tune: Mary Had a Little Lamb)

*A groundhog was in his hole one day, hole one day, hole one day.
A groundhog was in his hole one day and decided to come out.*

*He stuck his head out of his hole, of his hole, of his hole.
He stuck his head out of his hole, to see what was about.*

*He jumped back in so fast you see, fast you see, fast you see.
He jumped back in so fast you see, because he was afraid.*

*His shadow is what frightened him, frightened him, frightened him.
His shadow is what frightened him, it was so big and dark.*

*Now he's going back to sleep, back to sleep, back to sleep,
Now he's going back to sleep, for six long weeks to come.*

by Susan Spaete

GROUNDHOG, GROUNDHOG

Groundhog, groundhog, will you come out?
(Place thumb inside fist)
Yes sir, yes sir, if the sun is not about.
(Pop thumb out)
*Groundhog, groundhog, the sun is shining bright.
I'll hop back in and curl up tight.*
(Put thumb back in fingers)

by Susan Spaete

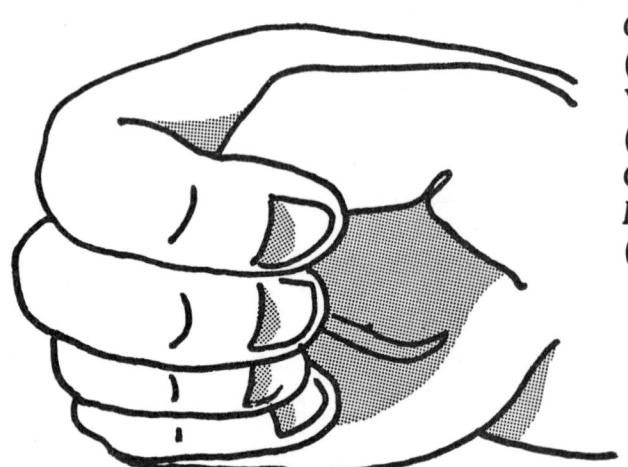

Story

• Read several stories about groundhogs to the children. WAKE UP GROUNDHOG by Carol L. Cohen or WILL SPRING BE EARLY by David Johnson Leisk are two suggestions.

ACTIVITY TIME

Art

• SILHOUETTE ART — When each child comes to art have him tear a piece of black construction paper into small pieces and put them in front of him. Then give each child a piece of white construction paper. He can use his pieces of black paper to collage any type of shadow he'd like.

• ME AND MY SHADOW — Have each child fold a piece of light colored construction paper in half. Using tempera, have him paint a picture of himself on one side. When he's done, he should fold the blank side over the picture and rub gently. After several seconds open the picture. *"Do you see your shadow?"*

Cooking

SHADOW SANDWICHES

You'll Need:

Favorite breads
Cream cheese
Peanut butter
Cookie cutters

To Make: Using cookie cutters have the children cut pairs of bread shapes. Then have them spread peanut butter on one shape and cream cheese on the matching shape of each pair. Put them in pairs on a serving plate.

Dramatic Play

• Get a large appliance box that the children can crawl into. Put several rugs inside to make it more comfortable. In a small box have three or four flashlights. Encourage the children to crawl into the box, shine the flashlight onto one of the sides, and draw silly designs and pictures with the light.

Language

• MATCHING SHADOWS — Put the matching pairs of black and white shapes from the *"Find Your Shadow"* game in a box. Have a piece of dark posterboard available. Have a child put all of the white shapes on the posterboard, then match all of them with their black shadows. When finished mix up the shadows for the next child to play.

• CHILDREN'S SILHOUETTES — Set up a projector in the area so the light projects against a blank wall. Have each child sit in a chair so his shadow reflects on the wall. An adult should trace the shadow of the child's head on a piece of black paper. As the adult is tracing she should talk aloud about the child's face. For example, *"I'm tracing around Stephen's mouth, now his cheeks, up to his nose, around his eye. What do you think is next, Stephen?"* Either the children or an adult can cut out the shadows. Put children's names on their shadows.

SNACK TIME

Snack

• Pass the plate of Shadow Sandwiches to the children. Have them take a pair. When everyone has been served talk about the shapes and their shadows. Enjoy eating them with glasses of chocolate milk.

Table Decorations

• Darken the room where the children are eating snack. Put flashlights on the table and in several other places to add some light. As the children are eating talk about shadows.

Place Settings

• Have small white muffin cups at each place. Fill them with snack foods that groundhogs might like to eat such as nuts, seeds, and raisins.

DISMISSAL TIME

Gather all of the Children's Silhouettes which you traced and cut out earlier. Hold each one up and see if the children can recognize whose shadow it might be. If they can, give it to the child and he can begin to get ready to leave. If not, tell them whose shadow you're holding, give it to the child, and he can get ready to go home.

VALENTINE PARTY

SPECIAL PARTY TIME

Because this is the first time most of the children have exchanged cards with so many other children, send home a class list at least a week before the party. Have the children bring in their valentines the day of the party. When the children bring their valentines in, have them put them in their decorated shoe boxes.

There are several ways to distribute the cards. Use 'Letter Carrier' or 'Immediate Delivery' if the children decorated their boxes with hearts. Use 'Mail Train' if the children decorated their boxes like train cars. (See Art)

• LETTER CARRIER — Have the children sit in a circle with their boxes in front of them and put their pile of cards to distribute behind them. The children take turns putting on a letter carrier's hat, putting their cards into a mail sack, and distributing them. If there are names on the cards the children might need help reading them. As the children receive their cards they may open them.

• IMMEDIATE DELIVERY — Before the children come to school set their valentine boxes out. As each child arrives, have him deliver his cards immediately. After all the cards have been distributed, have the children sit in a group, pass out the boxes to them, and let them open their cards together.

• MAIL TRAIN — Have the children sit in a long line connecting their train cars. The children take turns wearing an engineer's hat and distributing their valentines to friends. As the engineer is placing his cards along the track, the other children can make soft train noises. When everyone has distributed his cards, enjoy opening them.

CIRCLE TIME

Quiet Games

• LOVE WORDS — Talk with the children about the meaning of Valentine's Day and showing love to friends and family. Think of love words such as *'hugs'*, *'kisses'*, *and 'smiles'*. As the children think of them write them on a large piece of posterboard. When they are all written go back and read the list. Have the children turn to a friend and use the love words by giving someone a hug, blowing him a kiss, smiling at each other, and so on.

• WHICH ONE DOESN'T BELONG — Gather six or seven objects, such as a Valentine card, Valentine candy box, red ribbon, lace, heart necklace, pin, etc. which relate to Valentine's Day. Have three or four which do not. Put all of the Valentine objects and one unrelated object on a tray. Show the children all of the objects and ask them, *"Which one doesn't belong?"* When they guess ask them why that object doesn't belong. Have them cover their eyes, mix all of the Valentine objects around, and add a different non-Valentine object. Show them the tray and let them guess again. Continue several more times.

• REMEMBER — Put seven or eight Valentine objects on a tray. Show the children the tray. Point to each object and have them call out its name. Now have them cover their eyes. Remove one of the objects and hide it. Have them look at the tray and guess which one you took away. When they guess, bring it back from its hiding place, lay it back on the tray, mix up the objects, and play again.

• VALENTINE COUNTING GAME — Decorate a large Valentine Box. Cut several large construction paper hearts for each child. Write a numeral on each one.
    Pass out the hearts to the children. Call out a number. Have the children look at the numerals on their hearts. The children with the number you called out should come up and drop their hearts into the Valentine Box. Continue until all of the hearts are in the box.

Active Games

• **LETTER CARRIER WHISTLES** — The children form a circle. Choose one child to be the letter carrier. He walks around the circle holding an envelope. As he walks around the children chant:

*"The letter carrier whistles, the letter carrier sings
From house to house a letter he/she brings."*

The children continue chanting until the letter carrier drops the envelope behind someone. That child picks up the envelope and chases the letter carrier back to where the chosen one was sitting. The game continues until everyone has had the opportunity to be the letter carrier.

• **MUSICAL VALENTINES** — Cut a large Valentine heart for each child. Using red rug yarn or red tape make a giant red heart shape on the floor near where you are playing Musical Valentines. This will be your Valentine Box for the game.

To play, scatter all but one of the hearts in an open area. Play some music. As the music is playing, the children walk around the hearts. When the music stops, all of the children find a heart to stand on. The child not standing on the heart, takes one of the hearts off of the floor and goes into the Valentine Box. Continue playing until all of the children but one are in the Valentine Box. HINT: The children who are in the Valentine Box can clap to the music as they watch the children walk around the hearts.

Rhymes and Songs

ONE LITTLE VALENTINE

*One little valentine, two little valentines,
Three little valentines, four.
I'll cut and cut and paste and paste
And then make twenty more.*

FIVE LITTLE VALENTINES

*Five little Valentines were having a race.
The first one was frilly with lace.
The second one had a funny face.
The third one said, "I Love You."
The fourth one said, "I Do Too."
The fifth one was as sly as a fox.
He ran the fastest to your Valentine Box.*

Story

• Enjoy several Valentine stories, such as LITTLE LOVE STORY by Fernando Kraho or BEE MY VALENTINES by Miriam Cohen.

ACTIVITY TIME

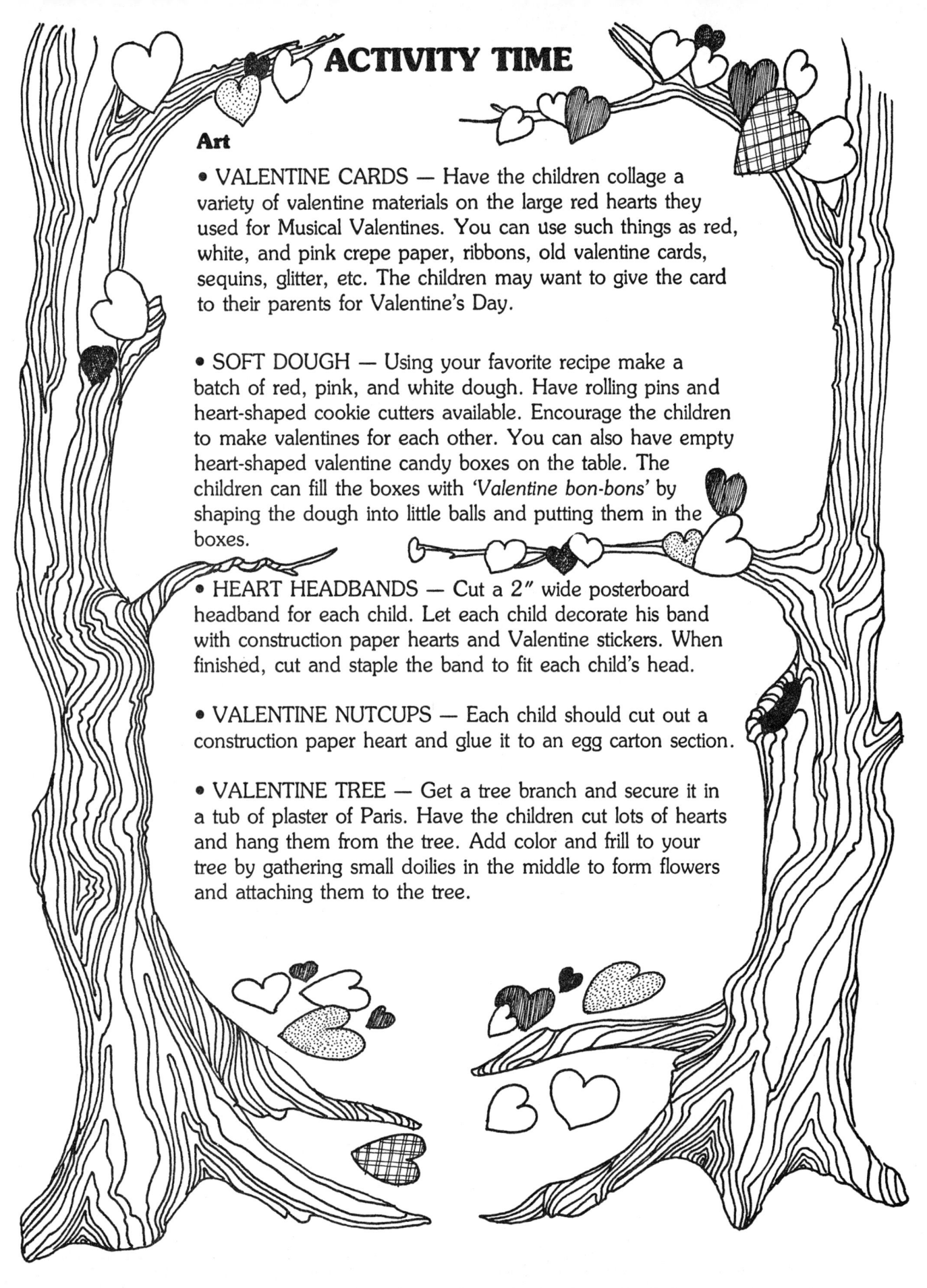

Art

- **VALENTINE CARDS** — Have the children collage a variety of valentine materials on the large red hearts they used for Musical Valentines. You can use such things as red, white, and pink crepe paper, ribbons, old valentine cards, sequins, glitter, etc. The children may want to give the card to their parents for Valentine's Day.

- **SOFT DOUGH** — Using your favorite recipe make a batch of red, pink, and white dough. Have rolling pins and heart-shaped cookie cutters available. Encourage the children to make valentines for each other. You can also have empty heart-shaped valentine candy boxes on the table. The children can fill the boxes with *'Valentine bon-bons'* by shaping the dough into little balls and putting them in the boxes.

- **HEART HEADBANDS** — Cut a 2" wide posterboard headband for each child. Let each child decorate his band with construction paper hearts and Valentine stickers. When finished, cut and staple the band to fit each child's head.

- **VALENTINE NUTCUPS** — Each child should cut out a construction paper heart and glue it to an egg carton section.

- **VALENTINE TREE** — Get a tree branch and secure it in a tub of plaster of Paris. Have the children cut lots of hearts and hang them from the tree. Add color and frill to your tree by gathering small doilies in the middle to form flowers and attaching them to the tree.

- **VALENTINE BOXES** — (Coordinate this with the Special Party Time.) Have the children bring shoe boxes from home. Using paper scraps have them decorate their boxes like train cars. Use heart shapes for the wheels. Another way to decorate the boxes would be to simply glue hearts all around them.

Cooking

VALENTINE SANDWICHES

You'll Need:

Bread or crackers
Peanut butter

To Make: Have the children spread the peanut butter on the bread or cracker and then draw big hearts on them with their index fingers.

Blocks

• DROP THE VALENTINE IN THE BOX — Make a Valentine box. Get a box and cut off the top. Decorate the sides with large hearts. Cut out seven/eight additional paper hearts. Have a child-size chair near the box.

As each child plays, he kneels on the chair facing backwards and tries to drop the hearts into the decorated box. When he's done he can take the hearts out of the box, count them, and then lay them on the chair so another child can play.

Small Muscle

• HEART MATCH — Cut matching pairs of hearts. Glue one of each pair onto a piece of posterboard. Put the mates in a heart-shaped candy box.

To play, the child should take one heart out of the box and lay it on top of the matching one on the posterboard. Pick another heart and match it. Continue until all of the hearts are matched.

SNACK TIME

Snack

• Enjoy the Valentine Sandwiches with the children's favorite red drink. You might have tomato or cranapple juice. Remind the children to wear their Heart Headbands.

Table Decorations

• Have several children carry the Valentine Tree they made over to the snack table. Put it in the center so everyone can see it while they eat.

• Have each child put his nutcup by his place. Fill each with nuts, raisins, and maybe a few candy hearts.

Place Settings

• At the children's places have white pieces of construction paper and sets of red stickers. While they are waiting they can decorate their mats with the stickers.

• Encourage the children to put one or two stickers on their napkins.

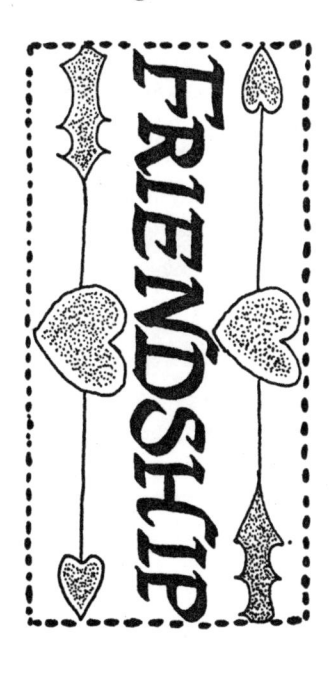

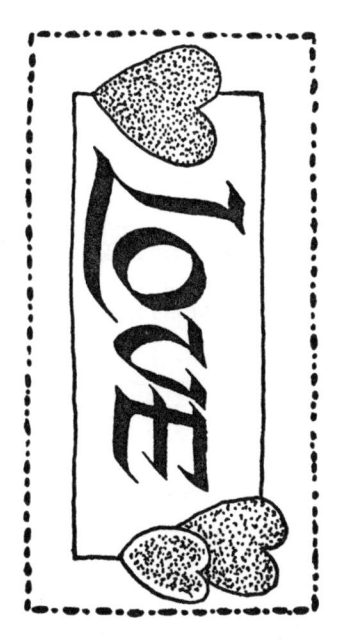

DISMISSAL TIME

Gather the children. Review what you talked about throughout the day — friendship, kindness, love. As a closing activity have enough *"Love"* coupon books to give one to each child. (To make the book, first write three different coupons — one for a big hug, one for a kiss, and one for sharing a job. At the bottom of each coupon write *"Pass it on"*. Staple booklets of these coupons together.)

Show the children a store coupon and explain how it works. Tell them that you're giving them a *"Love"* coupon book. They should take it home and give it to a special person. When that person gives a coupon back to them, they should give the person the *"Love"* treat (hug, kiss, sharing a job) on the coupon. Then the coupon can be passed to others they love and care about.

PRESIDENTS' DAY

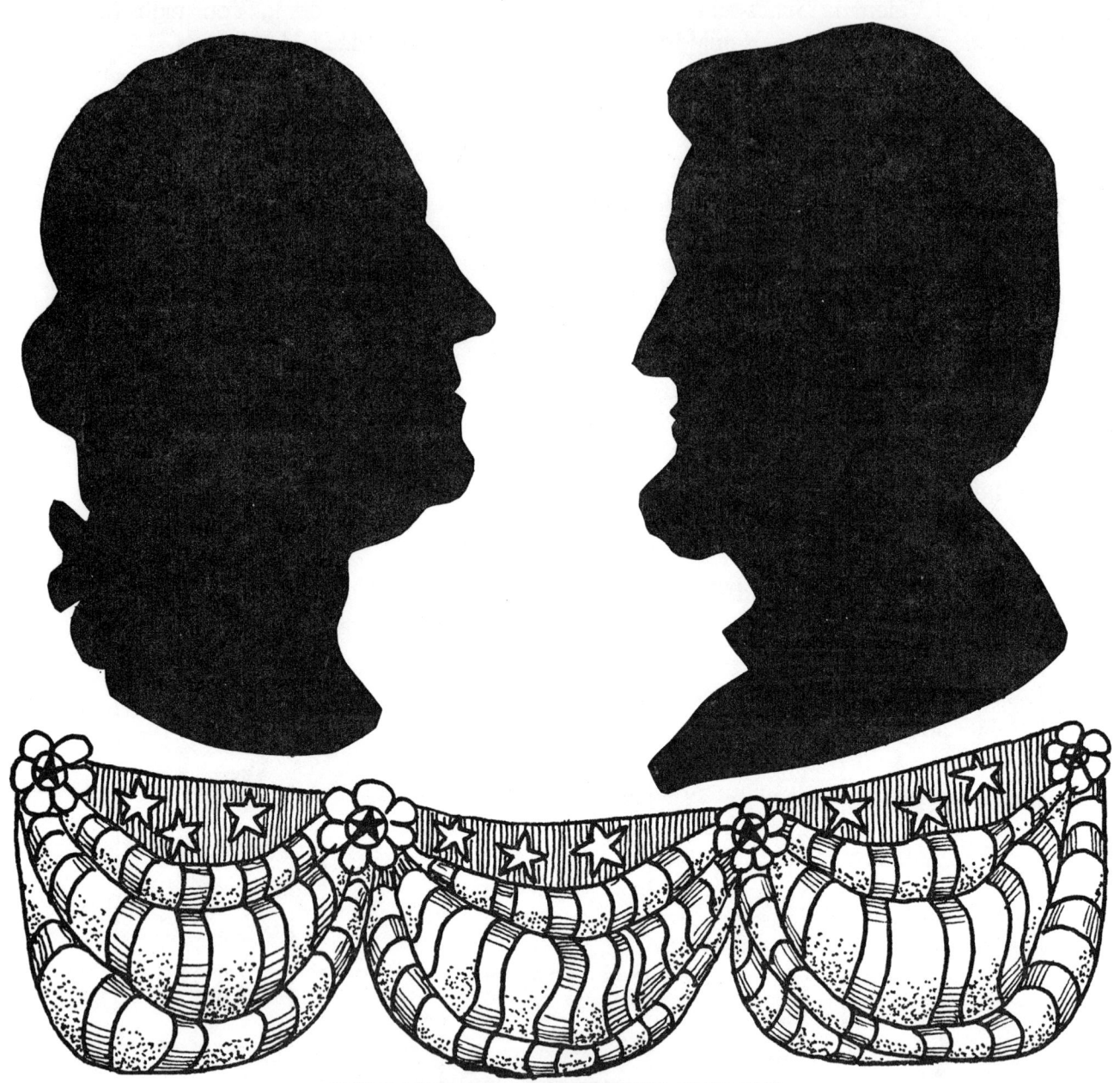

SPECIAL PARTY TIME

Celebrate Presidents' Day by having a parade with the children. Make each child a 3-cornered hat. Have a set of rhythm sticks for each child and a recording of *'Hooray for Mr. Lincoln'* by Miss Jackie from her Sniggles, Squirrels, and Chicken Pox album.

When it's Parade Time give each child a hat and a set of rhythm sticks. Have the children parade around and tap their sticks together as they chant, *"March, march, march . . ."* When they are able to march and play their sticks, put the music on and enjoy parading to the beat of *'Hooray for Mr. Lincoln.'* You might parade again letting the children sing as they march.

CIRCLE TIME

Quiet Games

• TALK ABOUT THE PRESIDENTS — Have pictures of the current President, Lincoln, and Washington. Show them to the children. Compare the three pictures, talking about things they see that are the same and different in each.

If you have a picture of the White House, show the children the President's home. Is their home like the President's home?

One way we honor Presidents is to put their pictures on our money. Show the children examples of money, including a Lincoln penny and five dollar bill, a Washington quarter and one dollar bill.

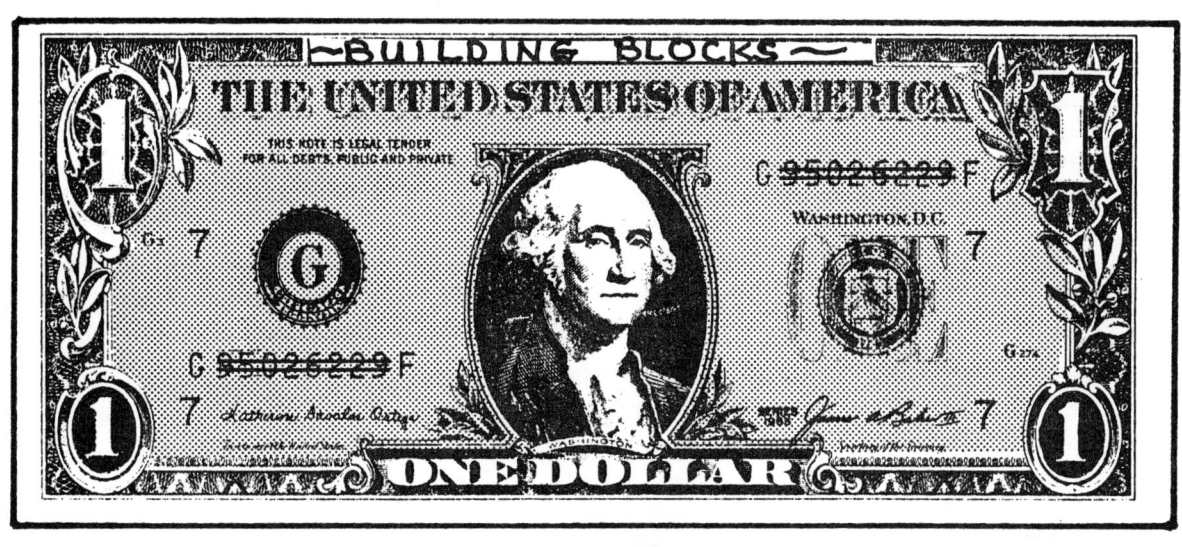

• **WHAT COMES NEXT** — Make seven to eight pennies, quarters, and dollar bills out of felt. Put a penny, quarter, and dollar in a row on the felt board. Point to each one and have the children name it. Now put a penny next to the dollar and repeat the pattern aloud with the children. Ask them what piece comes next. Put the quarter on the board.

Now pass out the rest of the felt coins to the children. As you say the pattern together, have a child come and put the next appropriate piece in the sequence on the felt board. Continue until all of the pieces are in order.

• **PIGGYBANK** — Have ten boxes with slits in them for banks. Write a number from 1-10 on each one. Have ten real or paper pennies for each child.

To play give directions to the children telling them how many coins to drop into the banks. For example, *"Cathy find the bank with the numeral 5 written on it and drop five coins into it."* As she drops them in, everyone should count the coins aloud. The game continues until everyone's coins are in the banks.

Active Games

• **MONEY DROP** — Have all of the children stand in a circle with their hands cupped behind their backs. One child has a penny. He walks around the circle and drops the penny in a child's hands. The child chases him back to his original place in the circle. Repeat until all have had a turn.

• **MINUTE MEN** — One child is a Minute Man and the others are British. The Minute Man stands with his back to the British. He closes his eyes. The British begin to creep slowly up on him. When the teacher says, *"The British are coming,"* the Minute Man opens his eyes, turns around, and tries to touch the 'British' who are rushing back to safety. Those who are caught are then 'Minute Men'.

• **STARS AND STRIPES** — Divide the class into three groups — stars (give paper stars), red stripes (give red paper bars) and white stripes (give white paper bars). Give directions such as:
— *"Put your star on your head."*
— *"Wave your red stripe."*
— *"White stripes jump."*
— *"Stars skip."*
— *"Red stripes hop."*
— *"White stripes get down low."*

• **FLAG SEARCH** — Buy 50 small United States flags. Hide them around the room. Have a large United States map on the floor. Say to the children, *"The United States is a very big country with 50 different states (name several), but we all have one flag. Today I've hidden United States flags throughout the classroom. When I say 'Go' hunt for them, return to the circle when you've found a flag, and choose what state you would like to display the flag on."* Continue until all of the flags have been found.

Rhymes and Songs

ABRAHAM LINCOLN

*Abraham Lincoln kind and good
Is honored and loved by many.
To help us remember this President,
We put his face on our penny.*

by Mrs. B. Lund

GEORGE WASHINGTON

*George Washington was the President who
Helped to start the red, white, and blue.
He fought in the battle to make us free
And guided our country to liberty.*

by Dick Wilmes

Story

• Read HAPPY BIRTHDAY by Dr. Seuss or GEORGE AND THE CHERRY TREE by Aliki.

ACTIVITY TIME

Art

• PLACEMATS — Let the children select a piece of red, white, or blue construction paper for a snack time placemat. Have them fringe their mats by snipping around all the edges.

• CHERRY TREE BRANCH — Have the children cut lots of small red circles from construction paper and then glue them onto a large tree branch. You can use this as your centerpiece for snack time.

• GEORGE WASHINGTON HATCHET — First have the children construct the handle by rolling a piece of white paper into a cylinder and taping it shut. Then they can cut a blade shape from red or blue paper and staple it to the handle. (If they make their hatchets before circle time they can pretend to be chopping down the cherry tree as they say the rhyme about George Washington.)

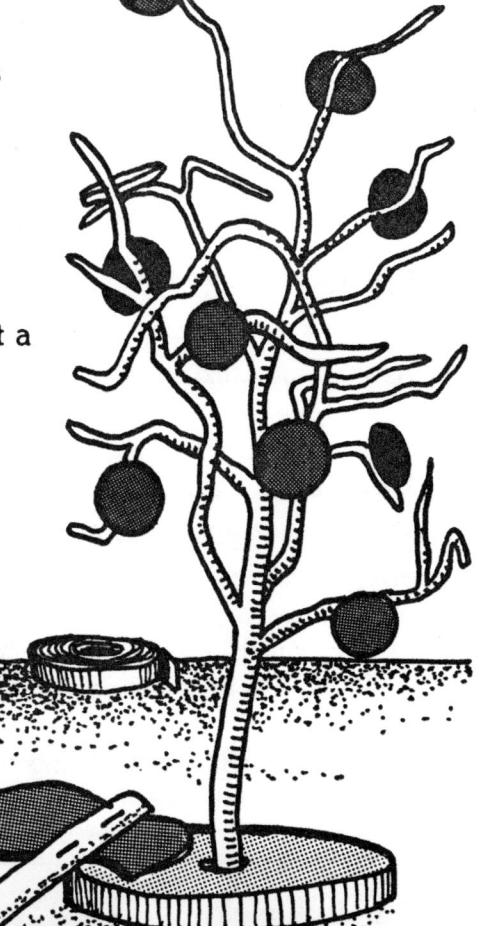

Cooking

CHERRY TORTE

You'll Need:

Pie crust stick
Cherry pie filling

To Make: Prepare the pie crust stick as directed. Give each child a small piece to roll out as thin as possible on a floured board or table. Place each child's pie crust piece in a section of a muffin tin.

Allow each child to scoop cherry pie filling into his pie crust. Bake at 400° for about twenty minutes.

Blocks

• LOG CABINS — If possible have several sets of Lincoln Logs for the children to use. As they are building, talk with them about living in log cabins.

Discovery

• CLEAN PENNIES — On your Discovery Table have a roll of paper towels, an extra plate of dirty pennies, and a bowl filled halfway with vinegar and a little salt.

Show the children how to shine a penny by dipping it in the vinegar solution and rubbing it with a towel. Once shined put it on the extra plate. They can continue until all of the pennies are shined.

• COIN RUBBINGS — Using double-sided tape, tape several coins to the table. Have crayons and thin paper available. Encourage the children to make rubbings of each coin.

Small Muscle

• COIN MATCH — Glue different coins to a piece of posterboard. Have a dish of matching coins. The children should study each one and lay it on top of its mate.

SNACK TIME

Snack — Enjoy the Cherry Tortes with glasses of milk.

Table Decorations

• Have several children lay the branch they decorated with cherries in the middle of the table.

Place Settings

• The children should use the placemats they fringed during activity time.

DISMISSAL TIME

Give each of the children a note for their parents. Tell them what it says and encourage them to enjoy the activity at home.

DEAR MOM AND DAD,

At school today we learned about Presidents. We also learned that some money has Presidents' faces on it. Please help me look through your change to match the pictures of money on this page.

WE FOUND

1¢

$1   5¢

10¢

$5   25¢

69

ST. PATRICK'S DAY

SPECIAL PARTY TIME

Before the children arrive make green leprechaun footprints out of construction paper, brush on glue, and sprinkle them with glitter. Tape the footprints in a path which leads all around the room and finally outside to a large *'pot of gold.'* (In the pot put a little present for each child. This might be a shamrock necklace with each child's name written on it.)

When the children come to school have them sit in a group. Talk about the symbols for St. Patrick's Day, especially elves and leprechauns. Draw attention to the footprints in the room. Discuss who could have left them, why he made them, where they lead, and so on.

Have the children stand up quietly, because you wouldn't want to scare the leprechaun, and follow the path. As you're tiptoeing down the path look for the leprechaun. All of a sudden you come to the big black pot. Let the children guess what is in it. Then quietly pull out each child's green necklace. Let him wear it throughout the day.

CIRCLE TIME

Quiet Games

• TALK ABOUT GREEN — Before the party send a note home encouraging the parents to help their children pick out green clothes to wear for St. Patrick's Day. Talk about the different green clothes the children are wearing. Tell the children that alot of people wear green to show that their family came from Ireland. Others wear green for fun. Have the children look around the room and find other things that are green. Walk over to a window and have the children look outside and find things that are green.

Hold up a green paper shamrock. Tell the children that shamrocks are one of the symbols for St. Patrick's Day. Ask them if they have ever found real shamrocks in the grass. If you have a shamrock plant pass it around for everyone to see.

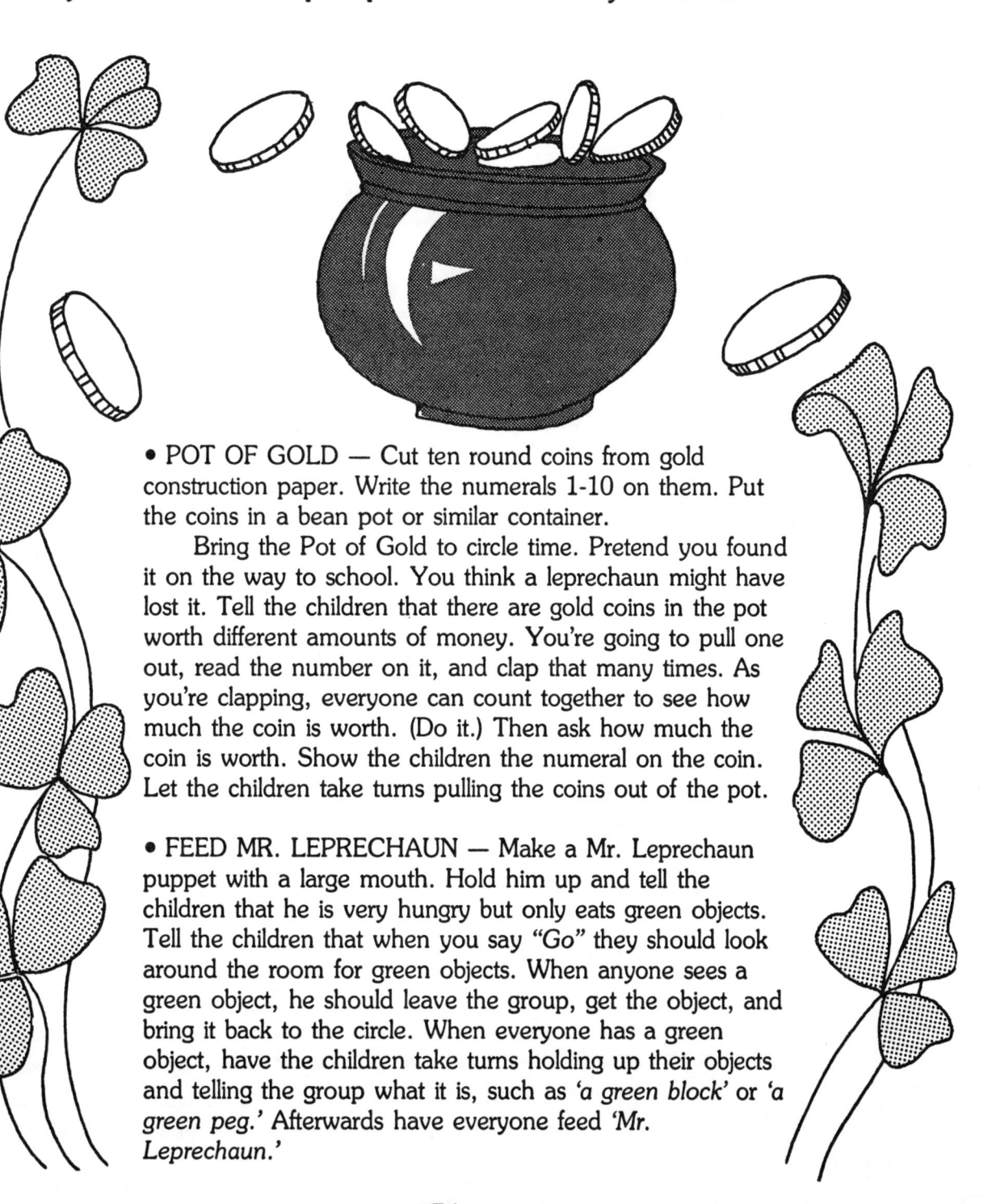

• POT OF GOLD — Cut ten round coins from gold construction paper. Write the numerals 1-10 on them. Put the coins in a bean pot or similar container.

Bring the Pot of Gold to circle time. Pretend you found it on the way to school. You think a leprechaun might have lost it. Tell the children that there are gold coins in the pot worth different amounts of money. You're going to pull one out, read the number on it, and clap that many times. As you're clapping, everyone can count together to see how much the coin is worth. (Do it.) Then ask how much the coin is worth. Show the children the numeral on the coin. Let the children take turns pulling the coins out of the pot.

• FEED MR. LEPRECHAUN — Make a Mr. Leprechaun puppet with a large mouth. Hold him up and tell the children that he is very hungry but only eats green objects. Tell the children that when you say "Go" they should look around the room for green objects. When anyone sees a green object, he should leave the group, get the object, and bring it back to the circle. When everyone has a green object, have the children take turns holding up their objects and telling the group what it is, such as 'a green block' or 'a green peg.' Afterwards have everyone feed 'Mr. Leprechaun.'

• BAKED POTATO — Using light brown construction paper cut at least one baked potato shape for each child. Draw a triangle, circle, square, or rectangle on each one.

Pass the potatoes out to the children. Have them look at the shapes on their potatoes. Ask a child to name the shape drawn on his potato. When he does, have him put his potato in the oven in the housekeeping area. Continue until all of the potatoes are baking.

If this is too difficult have each child hold up his potato and let the group call out the name of the shape. Then he can go and bake it.

• MR. ELF — You'll need a small bag for the Elf's gold. The children should sit in a circle. Put a chair in the middle.

Pick a child to be Mr. Elf. He sits in the chair pretending to be asleep. His bag of gold is next to him on the floor. Point to another child, who very quietly tiptoes to Mr Elf, steals his bag of gold, and quietly returns to his place where he hides the bag behind him. The child says, *"I've got your gold!"* Mr. Elf opens his eyes and tries to guess who stole his gold. When he does, that child becomes Mr. Elf.

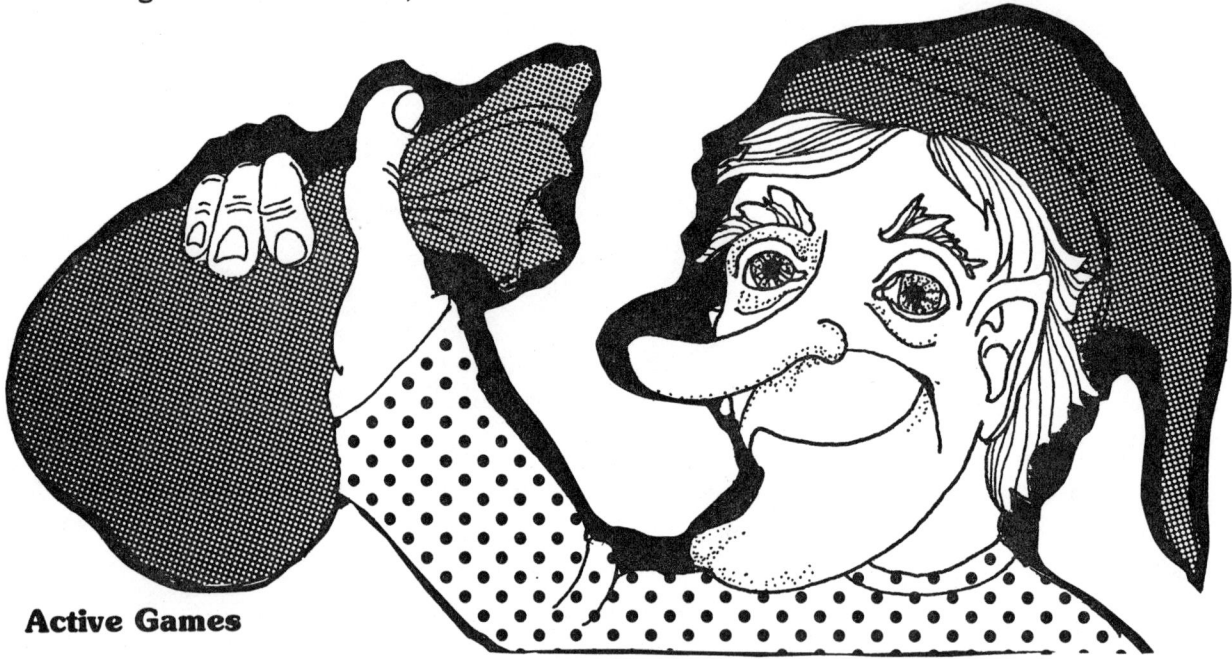

Active Games

• FIND THE SHAMROCKS — Make each child a headband out of posterboard strips. Cut three or four green shamrocks for each child. Just before the game hide the shamrocks all around the room. Have a stapler handy.

Give each child a headband. Have him put it on. Tell the children that when you say "Go" they should stand up and look all around the room for hidden shamrocks. When they find three they should bring them to you and you'll staple them to their headbands.

• HOT POTATO — Pretend a small ball is a hot potato. The children should sit in a circle. Give one child the *'potato'*. Have him roll it to another child. That child rolls it to another child. Continue rolling it to each other as quickly as possible because it is very *'hot'*. You can extend this game by having the child shout *"Hot Potato"* each time he rolls the ball.

• ELF, ELF, SHAMROCK — Play this game as you would Duck, Duck, Goose, except the child who is *'It'* says *"Elf, Elf, Elf,"* until he gets to the child he wants to chase him. Then he says *"Shamrock"* and runs as fast as he can back to the child's place who is chasing him.

- DROP THE SHAMROCK — Cut a paper shamrock. Have the children stand in a circle. Give one child the shamrock. He is 'It.' He walks around the circle and drops the shamrock behind a child and then runs. That child chases him back to the chaser's place. Then he gets the shamrock and the game continues.

- IRISH JIG — Get a recording of Irish music. Let the children free dance to the music or ask a parent to teach your children the Irish Jig.

Rhymes and Songs

FIVE LITTLE ELVES

*Five little elves sitting by a door
One found a shamrock, then there were four.*

*Four little elves up in a tree
One fell on his head, then there were three.*

*Three little elves, hammering on a shoe
One jumped behind a rock, then there were two.*

*Two little elves, dancing down the road
One found a pot of gold, so one was left, I'm told.*

*One little elf, left all alone to say,
Here is a wish for a Happy St. Patrick's Day.*

WEE LITTLE PATRICK

*Patrick is a leprechaun.
He has a sack of gold.
He hides it in a special place
Between two stumps, I'm told.*

*I think I once saw Patrick
Out in the woods at play.
He smiled and laughed and winked his eye,
And then he ran away.*

*Don't try to follow Patrick
To find his treasure sack.
He'll twist and jump and run away
And never will come back.*

by Dick Wilmes

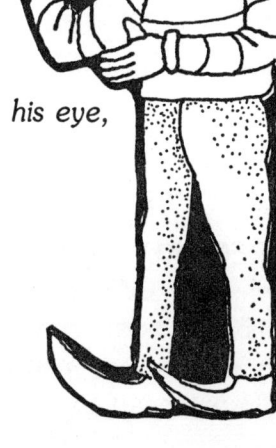

Story

- If time permits tell the story of the Elves and the Shoemaker and have the children act it out. You might want to read the story of the HUNGRY LEPRECHAUN by Mary Calhoun.

ACTIVITY TIME

Art

- GREEN COLLAGE — Cut a shamrock shape for each child. Have a box full of green collage materials such as fabric, yarn, ribbon, wallpaper, and snips of evergreen branches. Add green food coloring to your white glue. Let the children glue the materials to their shamrocks with green glue.

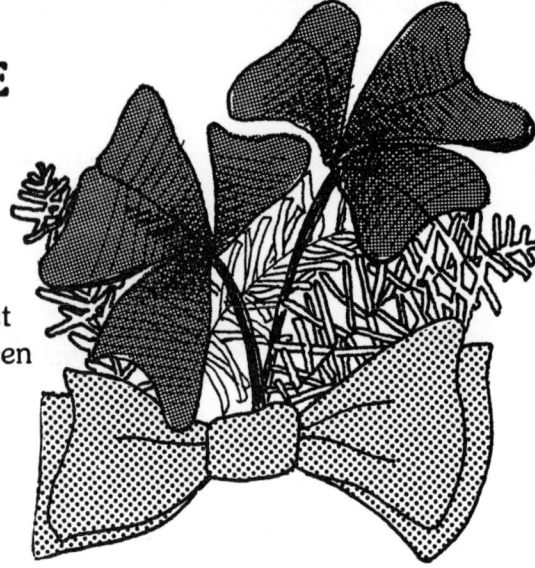

Cooking

IRISH BREAD

You'll Need:

2 cups flour
2 t baking powder
1 t salt
1 T sugar
3 T softened margarine
2/3 cup milk
1/2 cup raisins
1 T caraway seeds

To Make: Mix the flour, baking powder, salt, and sugar. Add the margarine and mix it in with a fork. Stir in the milk. Add the raisins and caraway seeds. Turn it onto a floured table and knead it until smooth. Spread it in a buttered 9" round pan. Bake for 30 minutes at 350°.

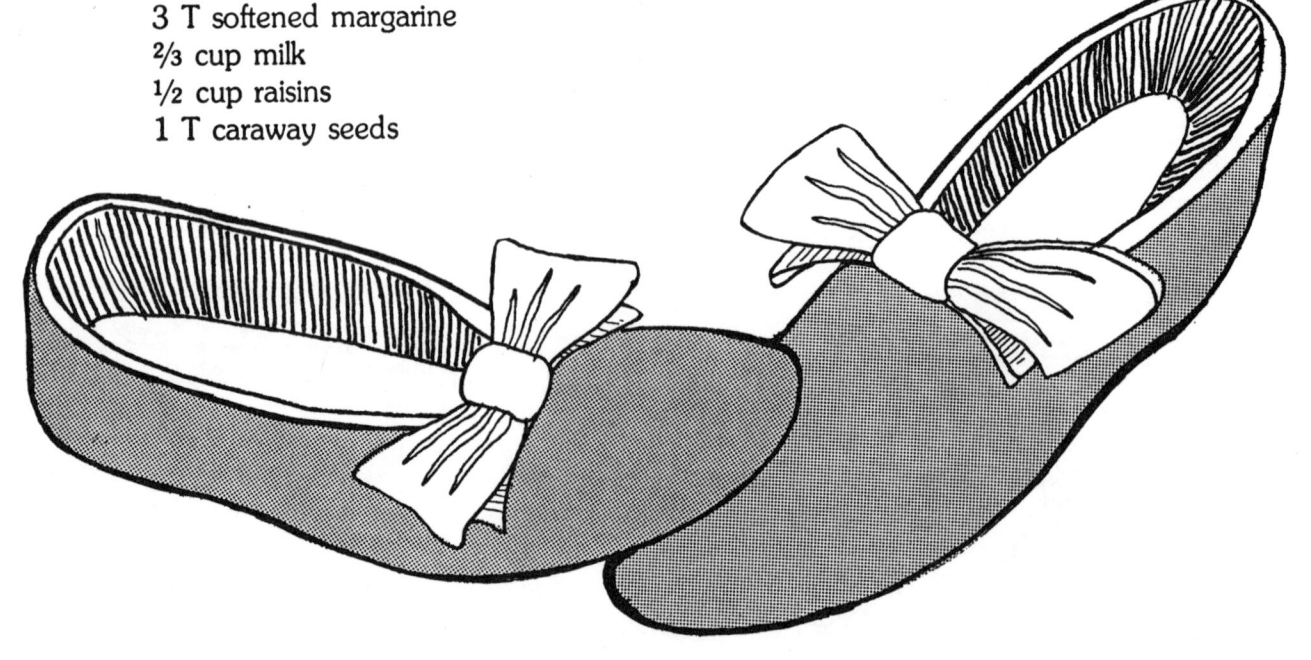

Dramatic Play

- LEPRECHAUN SHOES FOR SALE — Convert your housekeeping area into a shoe store which specializes in leprechaun shoes. You'll need different types and sizes of ballet shoes, shoe boxes, several rulers to measure shoe size, chairs, cash register, money, receipts, and so on. You might also make a large sign to hang over the entrance which says, "Leprechaun Shoes".

Discovery

• TASTE-TESTING THE POTATO — During the week around St. Patrick's Day taste test potatoes prepared in a variety of ways — mashed, french fries, potato chips, raw, baked, augratin, etc. Talk about which ways the children like them best.

• EXAMINING POTATOES — Cut several whole potatoes in half. Put the potatoes and several potato peelers on the Discovery Table. Let the children peel the skins off of the potatoes. What color is the potato after it is peeled? Watch it throughout the day. What happens to the color?

SNACK TIME

Snack — Enjoy the Irish Bread you baked along with glasses of limeade or milk shakes made with peppermint ice cream. If you couldn't make the Irish bread have several types of potato chips such as rippled, shoestring, and cheese flavored. Do the children have a favorite?

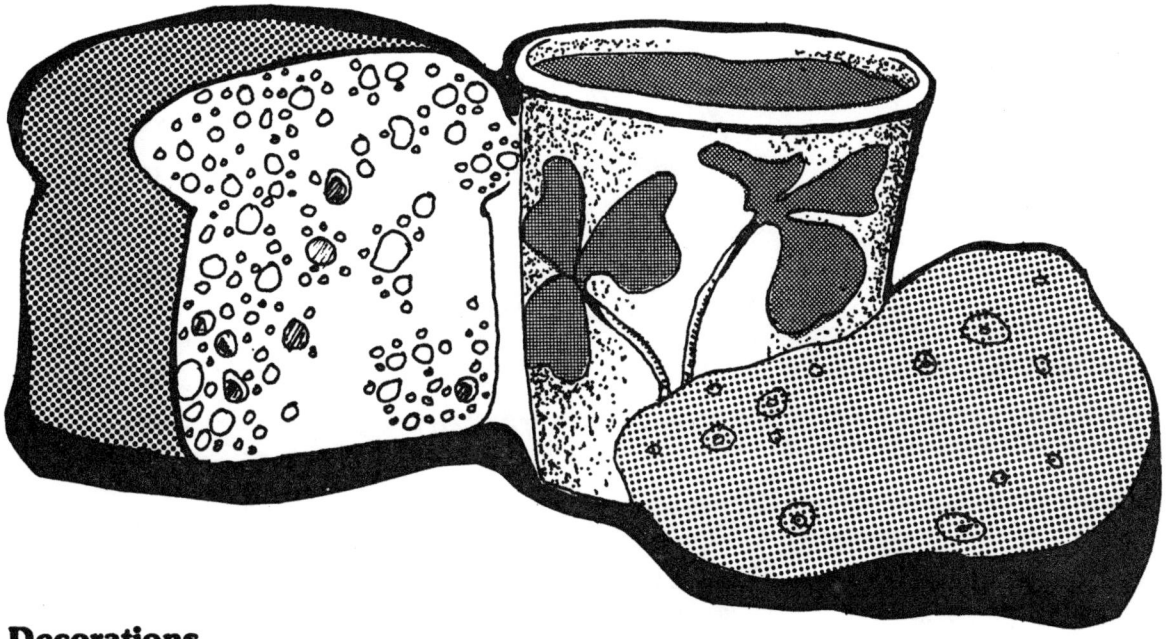

Decorations

• Have several small shamrock plants sitting in the middle of the table. You could also cut various sizes of green shamrocks from construction paper, staple them to green pipe cleaners, and have a shamrock bouquet in a black elf pot.

• Use small gold or silver aluminum foil muffin containers for your nutcups. Fill them with Cheerios®.

Place Settings

• Have the children use different shades of green construction paper for placemats. As you're eating talk about who has a very light and who has a dark shade of green.

• Put several St. Patrick's Day stickers at each child's place along with a white napkin. When the children arrive at snack they can put the stickers on their napkins.

DISMISSAL TIME

Get a real shamrock plant from the nursery. A large plant has several bulbs which are easily divided. Discuss the shamrock — its color, how many leaves it has, etc. The root of the shamrock is a bulb. Divide the plant and put one bulb in a plastic bag for each child. Staple on instructions for planting and care.

DEAR PARENTS,
 Here is a shamrock bulb for you. Just place it in a pot of soil to the top of the bulb. Water it when the soil feels dry to the touch. Soon there will be many leaves and flowers.
HAPPY ST. PATRICK'S DAY!

SPECIAL PARTY TIME

A day or so before the party have the children help you dye Easter eggs. Using crayon write each child's name on one of the eggs before it is dyed. Put all of the eggs in a large Easter basket.

On the day of the party, before the children arrive, hide the eggs in a room or outside where the children will not be going for awhile. Have the empty Easter basket sitting on the table.

When the children arrive, sit with them and talk about Easter. Show them the empty Easter basket and ask *"What could have happened to our Easter eggs?"* After discussing what might have happened, bring an Easter bunny finger puppet out to talk to the children. Have him tell them that he hid all of their eggs so they could have fun looking for them. They should stand up and follow him and he will lead them to where the eggs are hidden. Be sure to bring the basket along.

When everyone gets to where the eggs are hidden have the bunny tell the children how to look for the eggs and what to do with the eggs as they find them. After the directions, have the bunny say, *"Start your egg hunt!"* Let the children hunt for all of the eggs. When finished the bunny can say, *"All of the eggs have been found. Stop your egg hunt."*

CIRCLE TIME

Quiet Games

• EGG MATCH — Collect enough plastic eggs so each child can have a pair. Fill each pair with something which will make a noise when shaken, such as sand, pennies, peas, rice, beads, a ball, stones, etc. Put one of each pair in an Easter basket. Have the children sit together. Pass out the mates to all of the children. Taking turns let each child shake his egg so everyone can hear it.

Now have a child come up to the front, take an egg out of the basket, and shake it so everyone can hear it. Next have the children shake their eggs. If a child has one he thinks matches the sound in the first egg, shake both to be sure and then open them to see if they have the same ingredient in them. If so, pair them up. If not, keep shaking.

• FEED THE BUNNY — Decorate a gallon milk carton to look like a bunny. Cut a hole in the carton where the mouth should be. Pick a category which your children are familiar with such as colors, numbers, letters, or shapes. Cut out a bunch of carrots (several for each child) from orange construction paper. Draw a shape or whatever category you choose on each carrot.

Set the bunny on a chair so everyone can see him. Say a shape, *"Circle"*. All of the children look at their carrots. If they have one with a circle drawn on it, they should come up and *'feed the bunny'*. Continue until the bunny has eaten all of his carrots.

Active Games

• BROKEN EGG — Cut enough felt eggs for half of the children. Cut each egg in half in a different way. Keep them paired. Put the same numeral or number of dots on both halves of each egg.

  Pass the egg halves out to the children. Tell them to look at their eggs. When you say "Go" they should stand up and try to find the person who has the other half of their egg. When they do they should sit together. After everyone has paired off, have each pair put their whole egg on the felt board and read the numeral or count the dots on it.

• BUNNY, BUNNY, HOW'S YOUR NEIGHBOR? — The children should stand in a circle. One child is the bunny. He hops around the circle and stops at one of the children. He says, *"Bunny, bunny, how's your neighbor?"* The child answers, *"I don't know, but I'll go see."* That child becomes the bunny and the first bunny enters the circle. The new bunny hops to another child and the game continues. The last child goes to the teacher who says, *"Just great."*

• RABBIT TRAP — Choose several children to be rabbits. The other children form a circle, hold hands, and lift their arms. To start the game say, *"Go"*. The rabbits begin hopping in and out of the circle. After a little while say, *"Stop."* The children forming the circle quickly put their hands down. The rabbits inside the circle are trapped. They trade places with some of the children forming the circle. The rabbits start hopping again when you say, *"Go"*.

• BUNNY, BUNNY, RABBIT — This game is played like Duck, Duck, Goose. When the child who is 'It' taps a child and says 'Rabbit' the rabbit chases him around the circle until he gets back to the place left by the rabbit. Now the rabbit becomes 'It'.

Rhymes and Songs

FIVE LITTLE BUNNIES

*Five little bunnies, sitting by the door.
One hopped away,
Hop, hop, hop,
Then there were four.*

*Four little bunnies under a tree.
One hopped away,
Hop, hop, hop,
Then there were three.*

*Three little bunnies looking right at you.
One hopped away,
Hop, hop, hop,
Then there were two.*

*Two little bunnies resting in the sun.
One hopped away,
Hop, hop, hop,
Then there was one.*

*One little bunny wasn't having fun.
He hopped away,
Hop, hop, hop,
Then there was none.*

*Hop, hop. hop!
All gone away.
Hop, hop, hop!
They'll come back some day.*

LITTLE PETER RABBIT
(tune: John Brown's Body)

Little Peter Rabbit (fingers for ears)
Had a fly upon his nose (flutter fingers — point to nose)
Little Peter Rabbit
Had a fly upon his nose (same motions)
Little Peter Rabbit
Had a fly upon his nose
And he brushed it (wave hand past nose)
Until it flew away (flutter fingers)

2nd time — Omit the word rabbit (just motion).
3rd time — Omit rabbit and fly.
4th time — Omit rabbit, fly and nose.
5th time — Omit rabbit, fly, nose and brushed.
6th time — Omit rabbit, fly, nose, brushed and flew.

BRIGHT, SHINY NOSES
(tune: My Bonnie Lies Over the Ocean)

*Some rabbits have bright shiny noses
I'm telling you now as a friend
The reason their noses are shiny —
Their powder puff's on the wrong end.
Wrong end, wrong end
Their powder puff's on the wrong end.*

Story

• Choose an Easter story you think the children will enjoy. Here are several: THE GOLDEN EGG BOOK by Margaret Wise Brown, THE BUNNY WHO FOUND EASTER by Charlotte Zoletow, or THE EASTER BUNNY THAT OVERSLEPT by Otto and Priscilla Friedrick.

ACTIVITY TIME

Art

• BUNNY HEADBANDS — Using corrugated cardboard cut headbands to fit each child's head. Let the children cut ears from construction paper or textured wallpaper and then decorate them if they would like. Staple the ears to the headbands.

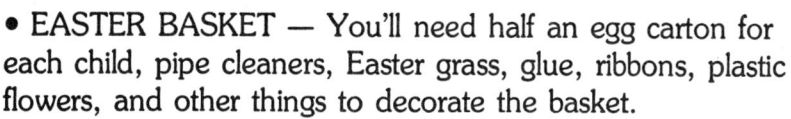

• EASTER BASKET — You'll need half an egg carton for each child, pipe cleaners, Easter grass, glue, ribbons, plastic flowers, and other things to decorate the basket.

Let each child decorate his basket as he wants. When finished he should add a pipe cleaner handle and a little bit of grass.

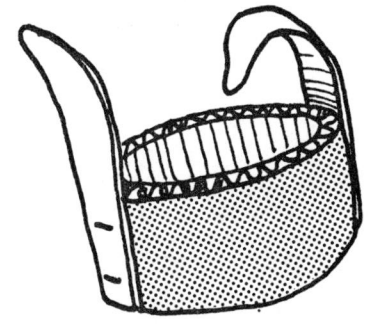

• NAPKIN RING — Cut construction paper into 2" × 6" strips. Have the children make bunny faces on their strips with crayons. Add ears by gluing construction paper shapes to the strips. Then glue the strips into a circle and let dry. Roll and insert the napkins into the rings.

• BUNNY PLACEMATS — Have pieces of white construction paper, cotton balls, black scrap paper, and glue available. Give the children pieces of construction paper. Have them make their bunnies by adding cotton ball ears and tails and black eyes to the white paper.

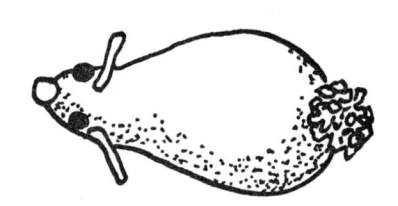

Cooking

BUNNY SALAD

You'll Need:

Lettuce leaves
1/2 pear for each child
Cottage cheese
Raisins
Red cherry bits
Carrot slivers

To Make: For each bunny salad, place a piece of lettuce on a plate. Put a pear on the lettuce with a scoop of cottage cheese for a tail. Add raisin eyes, a cherry nose, and carrot sliver ears.

Dramatic Play

• EASTER BUNNY'S HOME — Change your housekeeping area into an Easter bunny's home. The bunny is getting ready to deliver Easter eggs. Have several bunny headbands or costumes, lots of colored plastic eggs, and a variety of Easter baskets. You could also have other basket goodies, such as figures of bunnies and ducks.

Discovery

Set up a variety of egg experiences:

• CRACK AN EGG — Put an egg white in one bowl, the yolk in another, and the shell in a third. Place all three bowls on a tray along with a magnifying glass.

• DIFFERENT EGGS — Dye different size eggs. Put them in an egg carton and set them on the Discovery Table for children to compare.

• PREPARING EGGS — On the wall, hang a variety of pictures of different ways to prepare eggs.

• ANIMALS WHO LAY EGGS — Talk about egg-laying fish, birds, and reptiles. Get a variety of study prints from the library and post them in the Discovery Area. Enjoy the book, CHICKENS AREN'T THE ONLY ONES by Ruth Heller.

Small Muscle

• HUNGRY BUNNY — Draw ten bunnies each with a different number of buttons on his vest. Cut out ten carrots. Write the numerals from one to ten on the carrots.
    To play, the children should feed the bunny the carrot which matches the number of buttons on each bunny's vest. (Another way to play would be to have 55 buttons and the children match the real buttons to ones drawn on the bunnies' vests.)

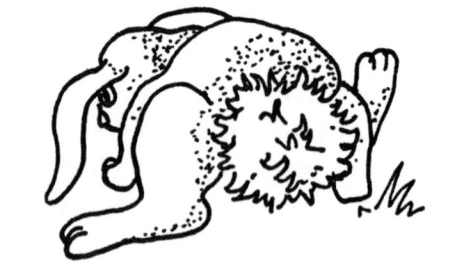

SNACK TIME

Snack

• Enjoy the Bunny Salad, Easter eggs from the egg hunt, and glasses of ice-cold pink lemonade.

Table Decorations

• Have the children help you make an egg tree centerpiece. Get a branch with several smaller branches on it. Spray it white. Secure it in a coffee can with a ball of clay. Cover the can with tissue paper. Hang paper eggs from the branches.

• Use the Easter baskets the children made at art for nutcups. Add a package of raisins to each basket.

Place Settings

- Use the bunny placemats the children made at art.

- The children can use the bunny napkin rings and napkins they made at art.

- Have the children's headbands at their places so they can wear them during snack.

DISMISSAL TIME

Have an assortment of six or seven plastic eggs. Put a picture or model of an animal hatched from an egg in each one, (fish, bird, caterpillar, tadpole, turtle, snake, and chick). Put them in a basket. Have matching animals to show the children. Put a Happy Easter note in the last egg and put it in the basket. (You may wish to have one Happy Easter egg for each child.)

Hold up each animal and talk about it. Now hold up one of the eggs, peak inside to see what animal it is, give the children clues about the animal, and let them guess what it might be. When they have guessed it, take it out, and put it next to its mate. Continue until all of the eggs have hatched.

— "This egg is on a leaf in the sunshine. It is a fuzzy, wuzzy CATERPILLAR."
(Open)

— "This egg is in the water with lots of other little eggs just like it. It grows legs and looses its tail. A wiggly TADPOLE which will be a FROG."

— "This egg is in a hole dug in the sand. The sun shines on the sand to keep it warm. Out comes a little TURTLE."

— "Here's another egg found in the cracks of a rock. This egg has something long and slithery in it. What is it? A SNAKE."

— "This egg is under a hen who keeps it nice and warm. Soon you hear a little peck, peck, peck . . . and out pops a fluffy yellow CHICK."

— "This egg is in a nest high in the tree. When it grows older this animal will like to eat worms. The ROBIN says, 'Wake up, you sleepy head'."

— "In this egg we have an animal who loves to swim in the lake and never needs to come up to the surface to breathe. Do you think it would be fun to be a FISH?"

— "I have one egg left for (each of) you. This egg doesn't have anything growing in it but it does have my love and wishes for a Happy Easter."

APRIL FOOLS DAY

SPECIAL PARTY TIME

A week or so before the party send a note home to the parents telling them that the children are going to celebrate April Fools Day by wearing their pajamas over their clothes. The day before the party, remind the children to wear their pajamas to school the next day.

On April Fools Day have a Pajama Parade. Have the children walk through all of the other classes and show-off their pajamas. When they get back to their room talk about all of the different pajamas everyone is wearing.

CIRCLE TIME

Quiet Games

• SILLY SENTENCES — Tell the children that April Fools Day is a day of silly events. Give them silly sentences in which they should fill in the blank.

"A _____ walks on his elbows."

"A _____ crawls on his head."

"A _____ sleeps on his tail."

"A _____ hops on his ear."

(Continue in this manner. Maybe the children can think of silly sentences also.)

• WHICH ONE DOESN'T BELONG — Before circle time cut out sets of felt characters which have two or three pieces which are *"normal"* and one that is silly. For example:

Three pigs without a hat and one wearing a silly hat.

Two cows standing upright and one upside down.

Several children standing up and one standing on his head.

Two wagons with round wheels and one with square wheels.

Put each set on the felt board. Have a child point to the one which doesn't belong in each set and then tell the other children why it shouldn't be there.

• DISAPPEARING OBJECTS — Put a variety of five or six silly objects on a tray, such as a clown mask, a comb without teeth, a candle that won't blow out, eyeglasses with a nose attached, silly putty, etc. Point to each one and have the children name it. Then the children should cover their eyes. Mix up the objects and take one away. Have the children open their eyes and guess which one is missing. After guessing bring back the one that disappeared. Play several times.

• TAILS — Get pictures of tails of different animals and pictures of the animals with their tails. Hold up a picture of a tail. Have the children guess what animal has that tail. Then show them the pictures of the animals. When you get to the one that has the correct tail, the children should shout, *"Tail!"* Then hold the tail and the animal next to each other. Do they match? Continue with the other tails and animals.

Active Games

• FOOLS TAG — Pick one child to be *'It'*. When you say *"Go"* the child who is *'It'* chases after everyone. When he tags someone, shout *"Freeze"*. Now the child who was just tagged and the original child who was *'It'* stick together. When the leader shouts *"Go"* the two of them try to tag another person. When they do, shout *"Freeze"*. The game continues with three children sticking together, chasing the others. Continue until all of the children are stuck together.

• SOUR PUSS — Have all of the children sit in a circle. They should have *'sour'* looks on their faces. Pick one person to begin. He walks around the inside of the circle and stops at one Sour Puss. By making funny faces at that child, he tries to make Sour Puss laugh. When the child laughs, he becomes *"It"* and finds another Sour Puss to make laugh.

• SILLY SONGS — Invite a guest musician to sing silly songs with the children. Have him begin with ones they know such as BINGO and then teach them several new ones.

Story

• Enjoy reading to the children I CAN LICK 30 TIGERS TODAY or PICTURES TO STRETCH THE IMAGINATION by Mitsumasa Anno.

ACTIVITY TIME

Art

• BACKWARDS NAMES — Before art write each child's name backwards on a piece of construction paper. For example, Susan would look like nasuS. At art have the children drizzle glue along the letters of their names and sprinkle glitter on them.

Cooking

APPLE SANDWICHES

You'll Need:

Cheese slices
  (colby or mild cheddar)
Large apples

To Make: Rinse the apples and wipe them dry. Remove the cores and cut the apples into slices. Put one slice of cheese between two slices of apples. Serve immediately because the apples turn brown quickly.

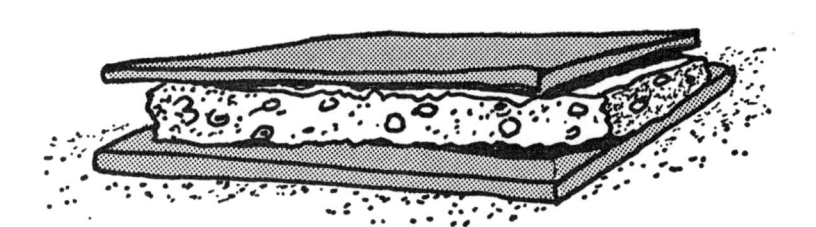

INSIDE OUT SANDWICHES

You'll Need:

Crackers
Cheese

To Make: Put a cracker between two pieces of cheese.

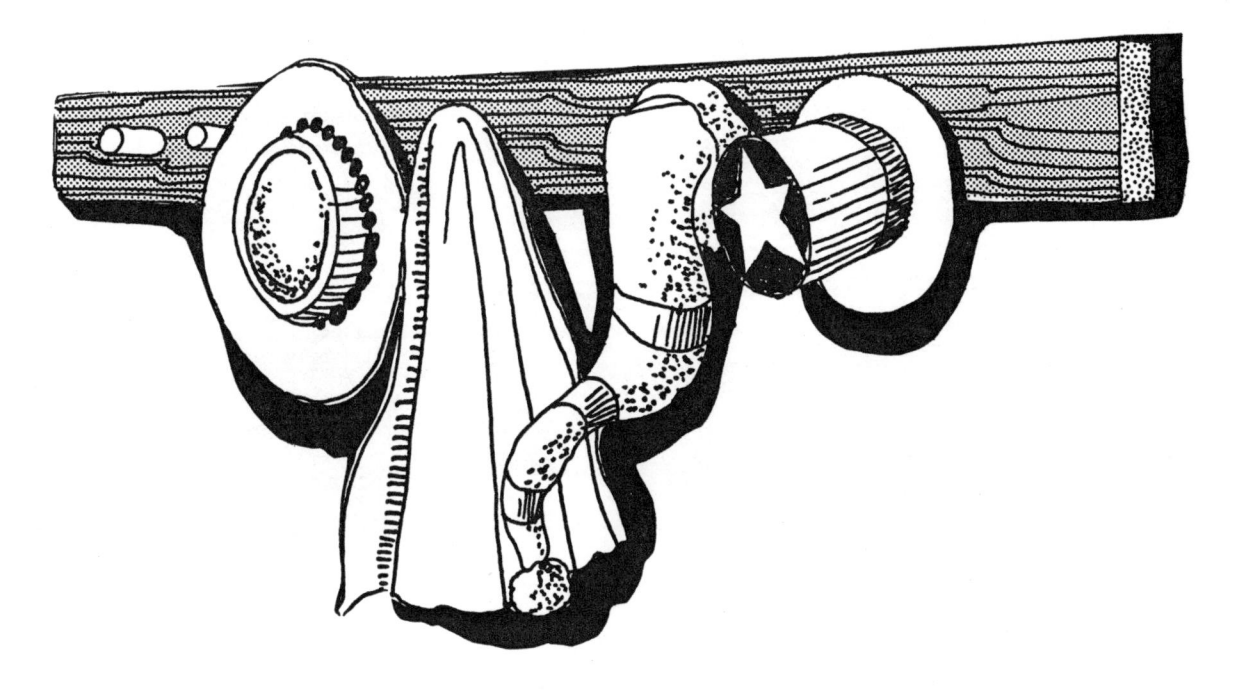

Dramatic Play

• LOOKING SILLY — Add silly hats and coats to the area along with extra hand mirrors. As the children are being silly, encourage them to look at themselves in the mirrors. Maybe they'll want to make silly faces also.

Small Muscle

• SILLY PICTURES — Get several silly pictures, such as one with things which don't belong, one with things drawn incorrectly, and one with people doing silly things. Cover them with clear Contact®. Have the children look carefully at the picture and circle the silly things with a water soluble marker. When each child is finished he should wipe off his picture with a damp sponge so it is ready for another child to enjoy.

SNACK TIME

Snack

• Enjoy the silly sandwiches you made during activity time along with glasses of blue milk.

Place Settings

• April Fools! Eat under the snack table today.

DISMISSAL TIME

Hold up the children's Backwards Names which they decorated at art. When they recognize their names, (help them when necessary) they can get ready to go. When they leave they should walk backwards out the door.

ARBOR DAY

SPECIAL PARTY TIME

The day before Arbor Day let the children paint a large cardboard box. When it dries add a sign to it which reads, 'Monster Trash Man'.

On Arbor Day give each child a little bag and take a Litter Walk around your school neighborhood. As the children are walking have them pick up all of the litter they see which is spoiling the beauty of the environment. Remember safety.

When they return to the classroom have the children drop all of their litter bags into 'Monster Trash Man'. Have the children wash their hands well and then look to see what a good job they did. Discuss what types of trash the children found around their neighborhood.

CIRCLE TIME

Quiet Games

• DISCUSS ECOLOGY — About a week before Arbor Day send a note home to the parents asking them to look through newspapers and magazines with their children to find pictures about keeping the world clean. They can also talk with their children about litter. On Arbor Day they should bring to school an article, picture, or story that they want to share. Have a special sharing time when the children discuss what they know about keeping their surroundings clean.

• DESCRIBE A TREE — Have the children go over to a low window and look outside at a tree (or have a large picture of a tree). Encourage them to think of as many words as they can to describe the tree. Write the words down as the children say them. Hang the list on your door so you can read the words to the children as you go in and out of the classroom that day.

• SPROUTING LEAVES — Cut four or five felt trees without leaves. Write a different numeral on each tree. Cut enough felt leaves to go on the trees.

To play, pass the leaves to the children. Put one tree on the felt board. Have a child (or you) read the numeral on the tree. Count to that number. Have that many children add leaves to the tree. Put another bare tree on the felt board, read the numeral, and continue as above.

Active Games

• SPRINGTIME FOREST — Talk with children about the different parts of a forest — grass, trees, bushes, flowers, nests, birds, insects, squirrels, other animals, and so on. After the short discussion, let the children choose what forest character each would like to be. After they've chosen, make up a story about a forest in the springtime. As you tell the story have the children participate by acting like the forest characters they have chosen.

Rhymes and Songs

PICKING UP THE LITTER
(tune: Paw Paw Patch)

Picking up litter put it in the garbage
Picking up litter put it in the garbage
Picking up litter put it in the garbage
To keep our world clean.

by Susan Spaete

FOREST WALL

Here is a tree (hands down at sides)
And here is a tree (hands out at sides)
And here is a tree so tall (hands over head)
Put them together with many more,
And we'll make a forest wall.

by Susan Spaete

WHO HAS SEEN THE WIND?

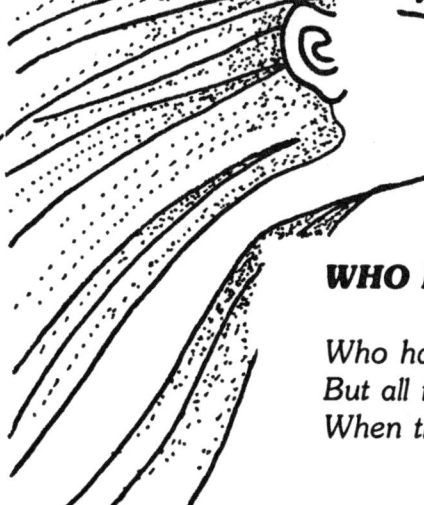

Who has seen the wind? Neither you nor I.
But all the trees bow down and sway
When the wind is passing by.

by Christaina Rosetti

(Read this poem to the children.
Have half of the children be the wind and blow,
while the other half are the trees which bend over.)

Story

• Read THE GIVING TREE by Shel Silverstein to the children. As you're reading it, ask the children to relate things they've done with trees. Are any of them the same as the child in the story.

ACTIVITY TIME

Art

• SPRING TREE — Draw a large outline of a tree on a piece of butcher paper. Cut a variety of sizes of leaves from sponges. Pour several different shades of green paint into shallow containers.

Lay the paper on the floor. Let the children sponge paint lots of leaves on the tree. As they're adding the leaves, talk about the different shades of green. Extend this activity by adding different colors of paint and other sponge shapes to print flowers and scenery around the tree. When dry, hang on your classroom door.

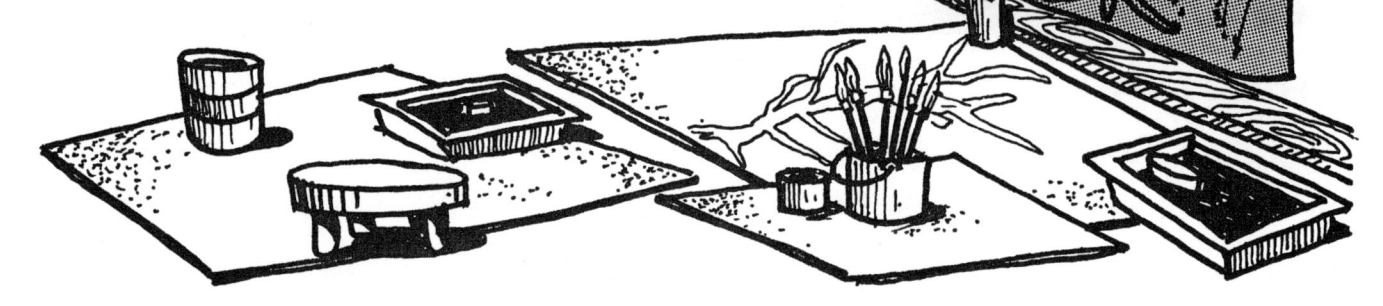

Cooking

ANTS ON A LOG

You'll Need:

Celery
Peanut butter
Raisins

To Make: Have the children wash the celery stalks and cut them into 2" pieces. Stuff each piece with peanut butter. Add several raisins to each one.

Blocks

• TREE STUMPS — Bring several tree stumps into the area. Encourage the children to examine them. Put out hammers, nails, and safety goggles. Let the children pound nails into the stumps.

Dramatic Play

• NURSERY — Turn your area into a tree nursery. Have garden tools, seeds, styrofoam cups, dirt, and water available. Help the children plant seeds in the cups, water them, and put them in the sun.

Discovery

- TREES ON DISPLAY — Place different parts of a tree on the table — roots, trunk, branches, leaves, needles, etc. Have several magnifying glasses nearby so that the children can see the detail in each part.

- LIVE PLANTS — Bring in a variety of live plants and small trees. Have the children look closely at the different types of bark on the trees. Which bark is the bumpiest? Smoothest? Thinnest? Do any of the plants or trees smell? How?

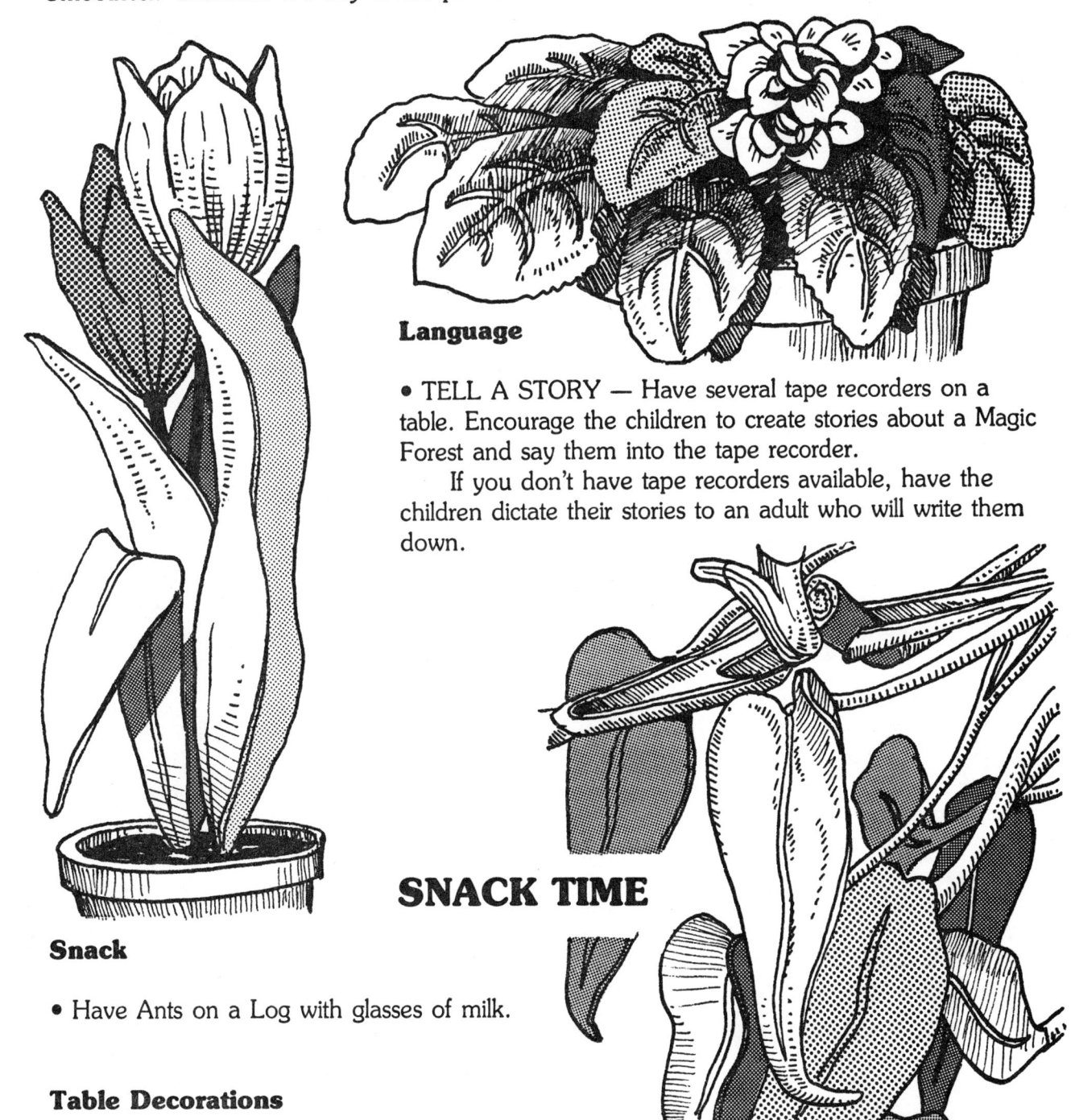

Language

- TELL A STORY — Have several tape recorders on a table. Encourage the children to create stories about a Magic Forest and say them into the tape recorder.

  If you don't have tape recorders available, have the children dictate their stories to an adult who will write them down.

SNACK TIME

Snack

- Have Ants on a Log with glasses of milk.

Table Decorations

- Have the children put several live plants down the middle of the table.

DISMISSAL TIME

Just before the children get their coats on, play or read the stories about the Magic Forest.

MAY DAY

SPECIAL PARTY TIME

Enjoy the May Pole Dance with your children. To do the dance attach one crepe paper streamer for each child to a long pole (broom stick). Have an adult squat down and hold the broom upright. When the music begins, the children holding streamers walk slowly around the pole, so that the streamers wrap around it. When it is all wrapped they can unwrap it by walking in the opposite direction.

Once the children understand the basic idea of the dance, they can do variations. You might have the girls walk to the music while the boys stand still and vice-versa or the girls walk in one direction while the boys go in the opposite direction.

CIRCLE TIME

Quiet Games

• MAY FLOWERS — Have the children close their eyes and picture a garden full of May flowers. Ask the children what colors of flowers are in their gardens? Are their flowers tall or short? Do their flowers smell? Talk about how flowers grow. What do they need?

• FLOWERS IN A POT — Have ten flower pots on the floor. Write a numeral from 1-10 on each pot. Have a bucket with 55 artificial flowers in it. Call on a child and say a number to him. He should take a handful of flowers from the bucket, go to the pot with the number you told him marked on it, and one at a time put the flowers in the pot as the remaining children count. If he has any flowers left he can return them to the bucket. If he needs more flowers he should get them from the bucket.

Active Games

• FLOWER POWER — Cut four different kinds of flowers out of construction paper for your children. Tape (pin) one flower to each child. When you say "Go", have the children find others who are wearing flowers that match theirs. When everyone is matched there should be four groups of children.

Now give the groups of children instructions such as:

"Violets, please walk to the door."

"Tulips, run to the window."

"Roses, crawl under the table."

"Daisies, tiptoe to the block shelf."

Continue in this fashion. You may want to expand this idea by grouping flowers and having two or three types of flowers doing the same activity, such as violets and tulips hopping around the room.

• RING AROUND THE ROSIE — Have the children stand in a circle holding hands. As they sing the song they should walk around. When the song says *"fall down"* they should drop to the floor. Do several times.

*Ring around the rosie
Pocket full of posie
Ashes, ashes we all fall down!*

• MAY BASKET — The children sit in a circle while one child sits on a chair in the middle. When the child in the middle closes his eyes, a child from the circle takes a May Basket, sneaks behind the person in the middle, and puts the basket down. After it is down, he goes back to his place, disguises his voice and says, *"Happy May Day"*. The child on the chair tries to guess who is giving him a May Basket. When he does they trade places and the game continues.

TULIP

ROSE

DAISY

Rhymes and Songs

PLANTING

*I took a little seed one day
About a month ago.
I put it in a pot of dirt
In hopes that it would grow.*

*I poured a little water
To make the soil right.
I set the pot upon the sill
Where the sun would give it light.*

*I checked the pot most every day,
And turned it once or twice.
With a little care and water
I helped it grow so nice.*

by Dick Wilmes

Story

• Choose a book about flowers and springtime to read to the children. Here are several:

THE ROSE IN MY GARDEN, Arnold Lobel
REALLY SPRING, Gene Zion
THE PLANT SITTER, Gene Zion

ACTIVITY TIME

Art

- FLOWER HEADBAND — Cut posterboard strips about 2" wide to fit each child's head. Have collage materials and glue available. The children can make flowers for their headbands and glue them on. When each child is finished staple his headband for him.

- MAY BASKETS — Cut three or four pieces of colored tissue paper into 4" squares. Have the children fold the pieces back and forth like a fan. Then staple them together in the middle. Pull each section of paper carefully apart to form the blossom. Place the flower in a cupcake liner. Add a pipe cleaner stem. Cut a leaf. Have each child (or you) write his name on the leaf and staple it to the pipe cleaner stem.

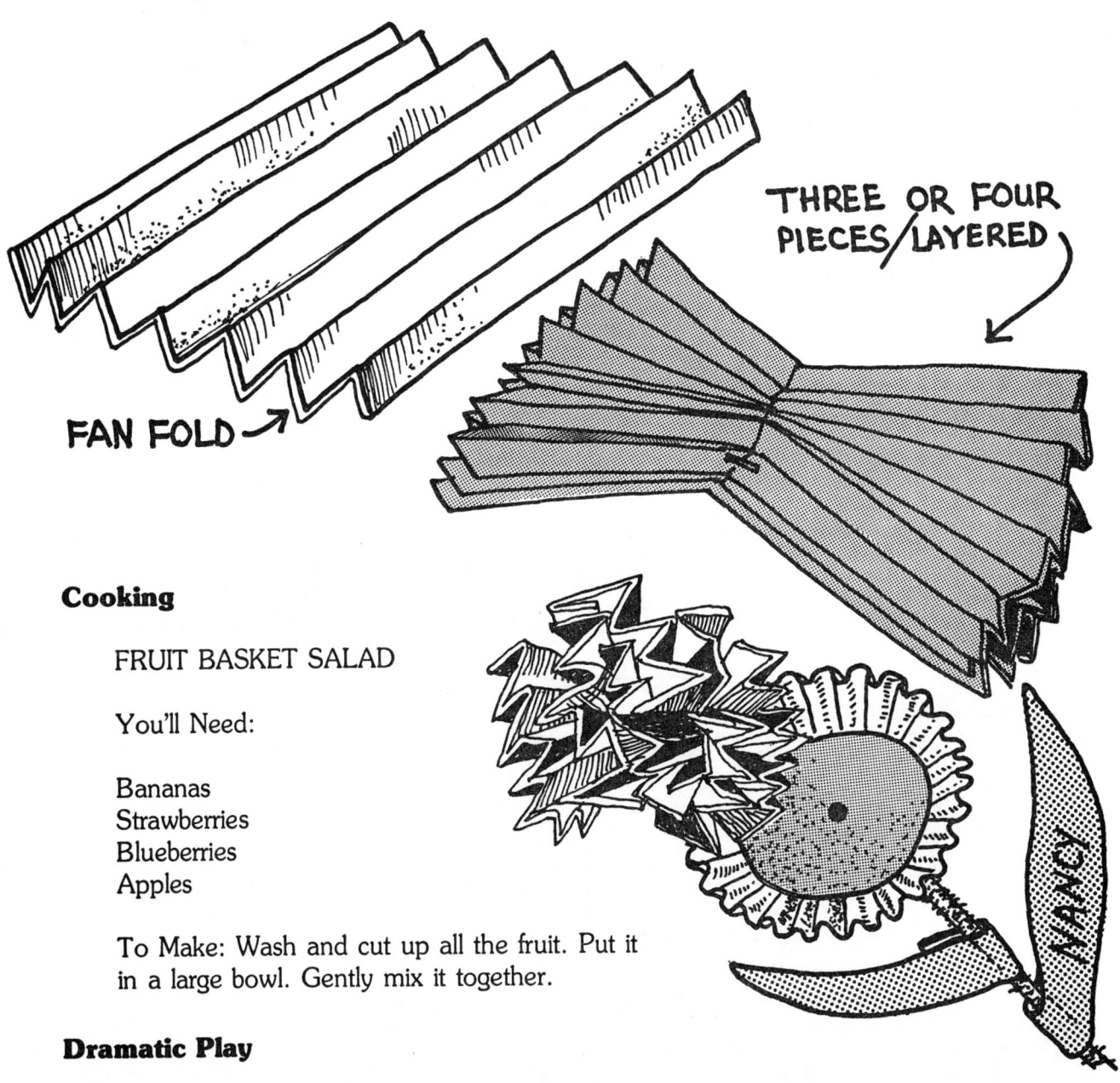

FAN FOLD

THREE OR FOUR PIECES/LAYERED

Cooking

FRUIT BASKET SALAD

You'll Need:

Bananas
Strawberries
Blueberries
Apples

To Make: Wash and cut up all the fruit. Put it in a large bowl. Gently mix it together.

Dramatic Play

- FLORIST SHOP — Convert your area into a Florist Shop. You'll need a variety of artificial flowers, vases, flower pots, a cash register, pads of paper, pencils, and tissue paper to wrap bouquets, etc.

Discovery

• CRYSTAL GARDEN — Make a crystal garden with your children. Put a mixture of 1/4 cup salt, 1/4 cup bluing, and 1/4 cup ammonia into a glass jar. Put four to six charcoal briquets in an aluminum pie pan and pour the mixture over them. Place it in a warm area. Watch the crystals grow. (If you want colored crystals, drip food coloring over the crystals.)

Manipulatives

• SEED MATCH — Get pairs of empty flower seed packages. Glue one of each package onto a piece of posterboard. Put the matching packages in a box. To play find the pairs and put them together.

SNACK TIME

Snack

• Serve the Fruit Basket Salad with glasses of fresh orange juice.

Table Decorations

• During activity time order flower arrangements from the Florist Shop. Put these arrangements on the snack table.

Table Settings

• Use pastel colored construction paper for mats. Place a May Basket at each child's place.

DISMISSAL TIME

Tell the children that they should deliver their May Baskets to secret friends when they get home. To deliver the baskets, they go up to the person's door, put the basket down, ring the doorbell, and quickly go hide. When the person comes to the door he sees his surprise basket waiting for him. Happy May Day!

PATRIOTIC DAYS

SPECIAL PARTY TIME

The day before the holiday decorate wagons, buggies, bikes, and other large vehicles with crepe paper and balloons. Park them inside so that they are protected from wind and/or rain overnight.

On the day of the party take all of the decorated vehicles outside. Have a holiday parade around the neighborhood. Wave to the people you meet along the way.

CIRCLE TIME

Quiet Games

• UNITED STATES FLAG — Cut red and white stripes, blue rectangles, and white stars so each child has at least two of the four parts in the flag.

Hold up a United States flag. Point to the different parts and have the children call out what section you're touching, such as a red stripe or the blue rectangle. Explain to the children that anyone who sees the flag knows that it is from the United States. Other countries have flags that are different from ours.

Distribute the red, white, and blue pieces that you cut out to the children. Point to a section of the flag. Have the children call out what you're pointing to and then those who have that piece should hold it up. Point to another section, have the children call out what it is, and then hold up the appropriate piece. Continue in this manner, repeating each section of the flag at least twice.

• STAR SEARCH — Cut one large construction paper star for each child in your class. Write the first letter of each child's name on his star. (There will probably be duplicates.) Cut a headband for each child.

Hold up a star. Have the class call out what letter is written on it. Ask, *"Whose name begins with _____?"* A child comes up, helps you staple his star to a headband, and then you staple the headband closed. He can wear the headband all day.

VARIATION: If the children know all of their letters and how to spell their names, letter enough stars to spell each child's name. Put all of the stars in a pocket chart. One at a time the children come up and find one letter in their name. They keep coming until they have found all of their letters. Staple the stars in order to make the headband and then staple it closed.

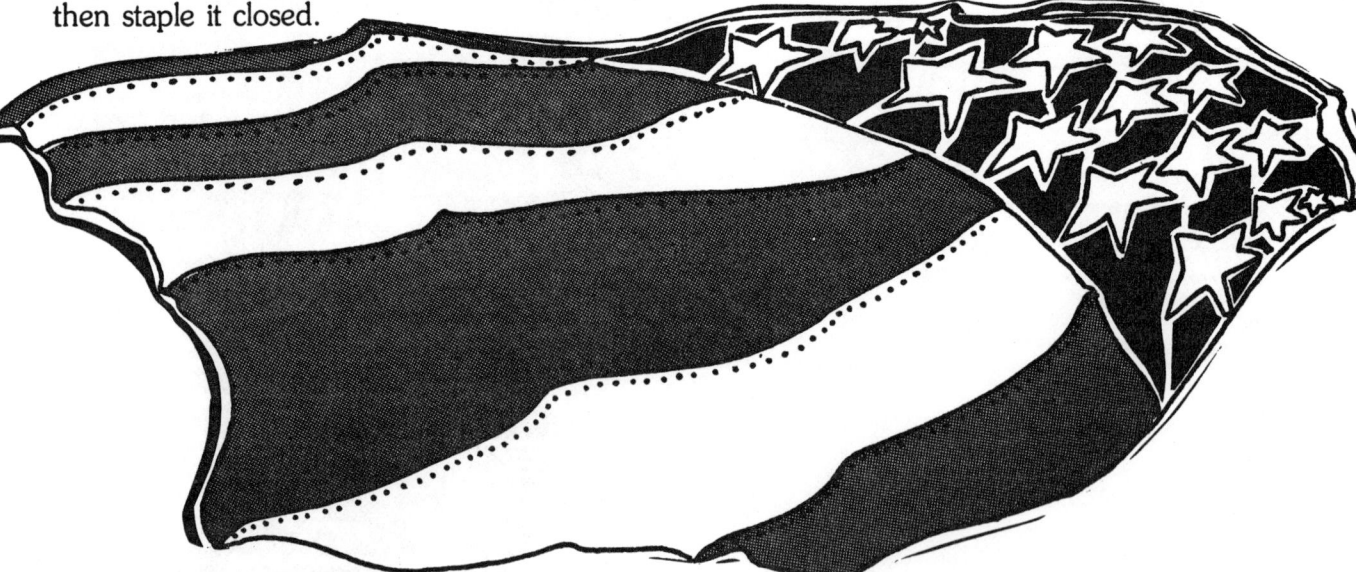

• PATRIOTIC PATTERNS — Cut two red, white, and blue construction paper squares for each child. Cut two red, white, and blue felt squares for yourself.

Pass the construction paper squares to the children. Using your felt board put a pattern of felt squares on it, such as red-red, blue-blue, white-white. Point to each square and say the pattern aloud with the children. Then have them make the same pattern with their squares. When they are done have them look at their pattern and say it again. Take the pattern down, put up another one, such as red-red-white. Have the children say it aloud, duplicate it with their pieces, and then say it aloud again. Continue with different patterns.

Active Games

Play these games outside at your picnic:

• MAZE — Set up a simple maze using trees, bushes, and other outside materials.

• PENNY HUNT — Toss lots of pennies into the grass. Have the children hunt until they find five pennies. As each child finds his five pennies he should help a friend find his five pennies. Continue until everyone has found five pennies.

• ENJOY FOLLOW THE LEADER — Have the first person lead the line in hopping, running, crawling, and skipping.

Rhymes and Songs

THE FLAG

Our Flag has three colors (hold up three fingers)
They are red, white, and blue
There aren't any others (shake head)
And we love it, we do! (hold hand on heart)

      by Susan Spaete

OUR FLAG

The flag is coming. We see it now,
It's red and blue and white.
With stars and stripes, it's held so high.
It's such a wonderful sight.

We are proud to hold our faces up
And stand so straight and tall,
To place our hands upon our hearts
And pray for peace for all.

      by Dick Wilmes

Story

• Read STAR SPANGLED BANNER by Peter Spies, A SUMMER SNOWMAN by Gene Zion, or DRUMMER HOFF by Barbara Emberley to the children.

ACTIVITY TIME

Art

• FIREWORKS — Let the children create their own fireworks show. Have them squirt a blob of glue on their paper and then using a straw, blow the glue around. When they've blown it as far as they want, they should quickly sprinkle glitter over the glue. Let it dry and then carefully shake off the excess glitter.

Dramatic Play

• DRESS-UP — Add red, white, and blue dress-up clothes to the area. Have several drums, rhythm sticks, and tambourines on a shelf. Encourage the children to enjoy holiday parades.

Discovery

• THE FLAG — Have a display of real flags or pictures of flags for the children to examine. You might also have several books about the United States flag on the table.

Language

• FLAG MATCH — Make a Flag Match game for the children. Make five or more United States flags except put only one to ten stars in each field. Cut out enough matching stars.

To play the children match the loose stars with those on the flags.

SNACK TIME

Snack

• Have an outdoor picnic. Serve hot dogs, chips, pickles, carrot sticks, and cranapple juice.

Table Settings

• Use a red, white, and blue tablecloth, cups, plates, and napkins.

DISMISSAL TIME

Ask the children if they will see a parade over the holiday. What do they think they will see — bands, clowns, etc? Remind them to look for American flags.

Tell them that many people take off their hats or stand when a flag goes by. Give the children flags. Let them line up in pairs and take turns walking by. Everyone should stand up. Remind them to look for flags as they go home or drive in their cars today.

BIRTHDAY AND A HALF

SPECIAL PARTY TIME

If a child's birthday occurs when school is not in session, such as during the summer, celebrate it on the child's half birthday approximately six months from his real birthday. Send a note home several days before the party reminding the parent to bring the snack for that day.

The birthday child sits in a special chair and wears a construction paper crown made from his favorite color. He may also wear an *"I Am Special"* cape. (The cape can be made from a piece of cloth about 12" x 18" and attached at the neck with velcro. Using fabric markers write *"I Am Special"* on the cape. Decorate it with sequins and embroidery if you like.)

While the child is sitting on the chair begin to make his birthday card. First fold a 12" x 18" piece of construction paper in half to form the card. With the child's help draw a birthday cake on the front of the card. Ask the child what color plate his cake is on. (Draw it.) Continue making the cake using the colors the child requests for the cake, frosting, and candles. Count the candles as you draw them. Then add the flames, counting those also.

Tell the children that you are going to put the card in the language center. They can draw a picture on the inside, write their name, and so on. The birthday child will then take it home at the end of the day.

CIRCLE TIME

Quiet Game

• STAR FOR A DAY — Have the birthday child sit in front of the group. Give him a large star with his name and age written on it. Pin it to his shirt. Have the children tell the birthday child things they like about him, things they know he likes to play, and so on.

Throughout the day the birthday child may make choices when appropriate, be the leader, and first in activities.

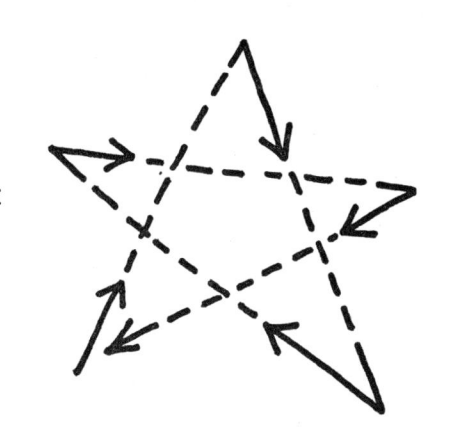

Active Games

• HIP, HIP, HURRAH — Act out this circle song as you sing the words to the tune *Farmer in the Dell*.

_____ (birthday child's name) *has a birthday*,
_____ *has a birthday*.
Hip, Hip, Hurrah, _____ *has a birthday*.

_____ *picks a cake*,
_____ *picks a cake* (child picks another child to be the cake)
Hip, Hip, Hurrah, _____ *has a birthday*.

CONTINUE:

_____ *picks candle one*, _____ *picks candle one*,
_____ *picks candle two, etc.*
_____ *blows out the candles*, _____ *blows out the candles*.

All children move back into circle.

Story

The birthday child can pick a favorite story he'd like you to read or you might choose to read JENNY'S BIRTHDAY by Esther Holden Averill or SURPRISE BIRTHDAY by Anabelle Prager.

ACTIVITY TIME

Art

• BIRTHDAY CROWN — Cut out a crown for the child. Using whatever medium he chooses, let him decorate it. Staple it closed to fit his head.

Language

• BIRTHDAY CARD — Have the birthday card, extra paper, crayons, markers, and pencils on a table. Encourage each child to draw the birthday child a picture on the card or on an extra sheet of paper. Some children may want to dictate a special message. Write down the words as they dictate.

SNACK TIME

Snack

• The parent brought in a special birthday treat to share with the class. Serve this with glasses of milk. Sing *"Happy Birthday"* either before or after eating.

DISMISSAL TIME

Give the birthday child his crown, star, and birthday card in a special Birthday Bag. Let him be the leader as the children leave for home. As you're all walking out sing *"Happy Birthday"* once more.

GOOD BYE PARTY

SPECIAL PARTY TIME

Before the last day make construction paper Award Badges for each child. On the badges write each child's favorite thing to do in the classroom such as *"Greg likes to build with the different blocks"* or *"Eric's favorite thing to do is paint at the easel."*

Gather all of the children around you. Tell them that you have really enjoyed being their teacher. You've liked watching them grow, learn, and play together. (Add whatever else you'd like.) Today you'd like to give them an award for their good year.

As you call their names, have them walk up to you. Pin the Award Badge on. While doing it read what is written on the badge. Then give each child a big hug and a thank you for a good school year. As you and each child are hugging, the rest of the children should give a big clap!

CIRCLE TIME

Quiet Game

• REMEMBER WHEN — Pick highlights which occurred during the year and talk about them.

— *"Remember when we played on the huge snow bank?"*

— *"Remember when Santa Claus visited our school?"*

— *"Remember when Mrs. Smith came to teach us about baby animals?"*

Active Games

• FAVORITE GAMES — Talk with the children about different games they enjoyed playing. Pick several favorites and play them one more time.

• FRIEND OF MINE — Have the children form a circle and hold hands. Teach them this good-bye song, sung to the tune of *Mary Had a Little Lamb*.

*(Child's Name) is a friend of mine, friend of mine, friend of mine.
(Child's Name) is a friend of mine. Good-bye (Child's Name.)*

Pick one child to go into the middle of the circle. Begin singing using that child's name. As the children sing have them hold hands and walk around the circle. When they get to the *"Good-bye"* part they should stop and wave at the person in the middle. The person in the middle picks another child to join him in the middle. Everyone sings to the second child. This continues until everyone is in the middle. Now give each other big hugs.

Fingerplays

Enjoy favorite ones the children have requested.

Story

• The children may choose several favorite stories for the teacher to read. The teacher may also tell a story that she has made up about her class.

ACTIVITY TIME

Art

• BUDDY PAINTING — Clip two pieces of paper side by side on the easel. When a child comes to the easel he should bring a friend along. They can each paint a picture while sharing conversation.

• FRIENDSHIP BANDS — Cut a headband to fit each child's head. Trace each child's hand about five or six times on a piece of construction paper. Have the children cut their hands out and put their names on them. They should staple one of their hands onto their headband. They can trade their other hands with friends. (Cut more if necessary.) As they trade, they should staple the different hands to their bands. They can wear these Friendship Bands all day.

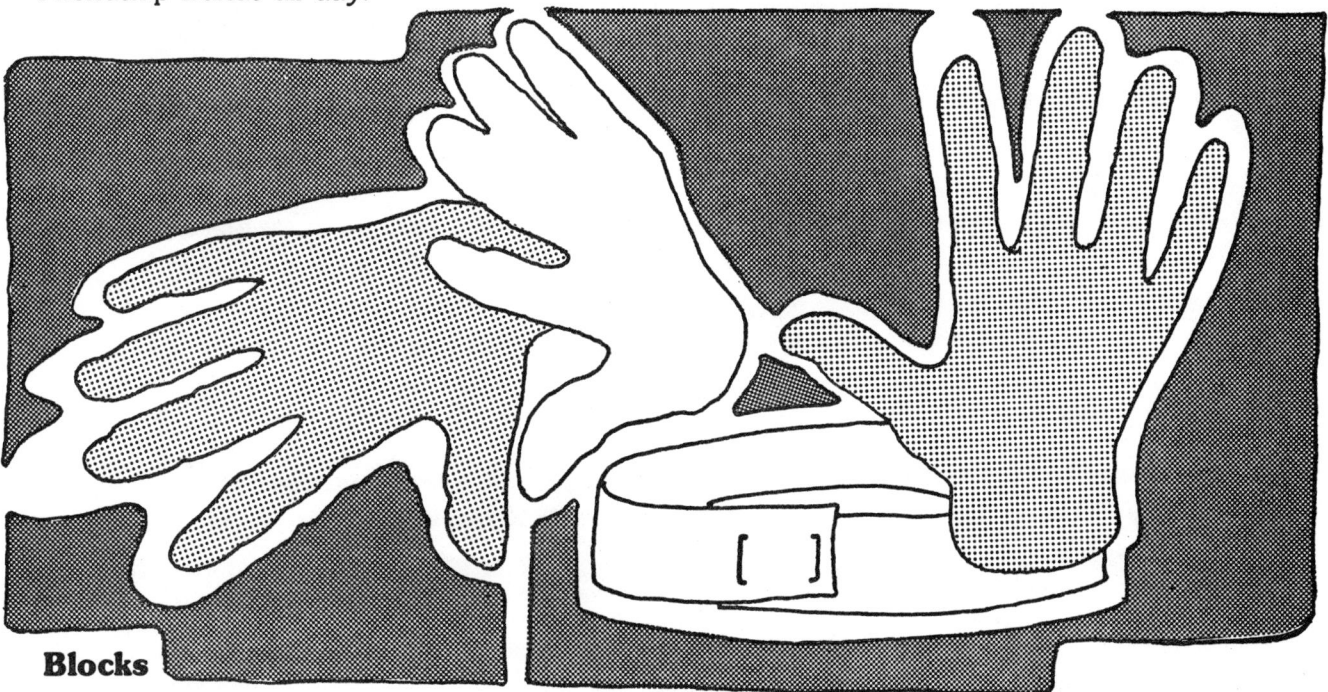

Blocks

• MAZE — Create a maze in the area using the climber, balance beam, inner tubes, large blocks, and other favorite pieces of equipment.

Dramatic Play

• BATH TIME — Let the children give their dolls a bath. Put two large rubber tubs half full of water in the area. One should have a little soap in it, the other one should be clear. Have several towels and wash cloths.

Language

• MEMORIES — On a table have photographs of different events which took place during the year along with several tape recorders. Have the children pick different photos and tell about them into the tape recorder.

SNACK TIME

Snack

- Have cookies made in the shape of hands along with glasses of juice.

Table Decorations

- Make a Good-bye Banner. Cut out two construction paper hands. Glue a popsicle stick to each one. Stick them in two balls of clay. Make a banner which reads *"Good-bye"*. Glue each end of the banner to a popsicle stick. Place it down the middle of the table.

Place Settings

- Make nutcups out of cupcake liners. Put nuts, raisins, and pretzels in each one.

DISMISSAL TIME

Sing the Good-bye song several times. Give each other more hugs and wishes for a good summer.

Good-bye, good-bye to you and you and you.
Good-bye, good-bye, may summer be fun for you.

FAVORITE THEMES

FAVORITE SNACKS

FAVORITE GAMES

FAVORITE SONGS AND RHYMES

FOR EVERY MONTH

BUILDING BLOCKS

an activity newspaper for adults and their young children

TAKE A LOOK AT BUILDING BLOCKS NEWSPAPER

PUBLISHED:
10 times a year including an expanded summer issue.

RATES:
1 Year ~ $20.00
2 Years ~ $36.50
3 Years ~ $50.00
Sample ~ $ 3.00

SEND YOUR NAME, ADDRESS (INCLUDING ZIP CODE), AND PAYMENT TO:

BUILDING BLOCKS
38W567 Brindlewood
Elgin, Il   60123

BUILDING BLOCKS is a 20 page early childhood activity newspaper offering a total curriculum resource to use in your classroom and share with your parents.

MONTHLY FEATURES include:

~ Reproducible parent activity calendar.

~ Activity pages highlighting language, art, physical, science/math, creative, and self/social activities which are easy to plan and implement.

~ Ready-to-use charts, games, and/or posters.

~ Special activity page for toddlers and twos.

~ Large easy-to-use illustrations.

~ 4 page **FEATURED TOPIC** *Pull-Out Section*.

Building Blocks

Felt Board Fun
by Liz and Dick Wilmes. Make your felt board come alive. Discover how versatile it is as the children become involved with a wide range of activities. This unique book has over 150 ideas with accompanying patterns.
ISBN 0-943452-02-3 $14.95

Parachute Play
by Liz and Dick Wilmes. A year 'round approach to one of the most versatile pieces of large muscle equipment. Starting with basic techniques, PARACHUTE PLAY provides over 100 activities to use with your parachute.
ISBN 0-943452-03-1 $ 7.95

Exploring Art
by Liz and Dick Wilmes. EXPLORING ART is divided by months. Over 250 art ideas for paint, chalk, doughs, scissors, and more. Easy to set-up in your classroom.
ISBN 0-943452-05-8 $16.95

Everyday Bulletin Boards
by Wilmes and Moehling. Features borders, murals, backgrounds, and other open-ended art to display on your bulletin board. Plus board ideas with patterns, which teachers can make and use to enhance their curriculum.
ISBN 0-943452-09-0 $ 8.95

Gifts, Cards, and Wraps
by Wilmes and Zavodsky. Help the children sparkle with the excitement of gift-giving. Filled with thoughtful gifts, unique wraps, and special cards which the children can make and give. They're sure to bring smiles.
ISBN 0-943452-06-6 $ 7.95

Imagination Stretchers
by Liz and Dick Wilmes. Perfect for whole language. Over 400 conversation starters for creative discussions, simple lists, and beginning dictation and writing.
ISBN 0-943452-04-X $ 6.95

Parent Programs and Open Houses
by Susan Spaete. Filled with a wide variety of year 'round presentations, pre-registration ideas, open houses, and end-of-the-year gatherings. All involve the children from the planning stages through the programs.
ISBN 0-943452-08-2 $ 9.95

Classroom Parties.
by Susan Spaete. Each party plan suggests decorations, trimmings, and snacks which the children can easily make to set a festive mood. Choose from games, songs, art activities, stories, and related experiences which will add to the spirit and fun.
ISBN 0-943452-07-4 $ 8.95

Circle Time Book

by Liz and Dick Wilmes. CIRCLE TIME BOOK captures the spirit of 39 seasons and holidays. The big book is filled with more than 400 circle time activities, including fingerplays, language activities, active games, and more.
ISBN 0-943452-00-7 $ 9.95

Everyday Circle Times

by Liz and Dick Wilmes. Over 900 ideas for Circle Time! Choose activities from 48 different topics divided into seven sections: self-concept, concepts, animals, foods, science, occupations, and recreation.
ISBN 0-943452-01-5 $14.95

Yearful of Circle Times

by Liz and Dick Wilmes. YEARFUL is the third book in the **Circle Times** series. It highlights 52 more topics to use on a weekly/seasonal basis or mixed and matched according to your curriculum. A perfect companion to CIRCLE TIME BOOK and EVERYDAY CIRCLE TIMES.
ISBN 0-943452-10-4 $14.95

Learning Centers

by Liz and Dick Wilmes. Hundreds of open-ended activities to quickly involve and excite your children. You'll use it every time you plan and whenever you need a quick, additional activity. A must for every teacher's bookshelf.
ISBN 0-943452-13-9 $16.95

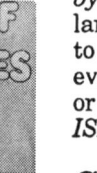

Make-Take Games

by Liz and Dick Wilmes. Features 32 large, colorful games which are easy to make. Children will have fun everyday playing them by themselves or in groups.
ISBN 0-943452-11-2 $12.95

Companion Pattern Set

Game-making made even easier! Set of 21 posterboard size sheets to accompany MAKE-TAKE GAMES. Ready-to-use, a great time saver. Plus use the patterns for other activities which need a visual aid.
ISBN 0-943452-12-0 $24.95
Large 22"x28" Sheets

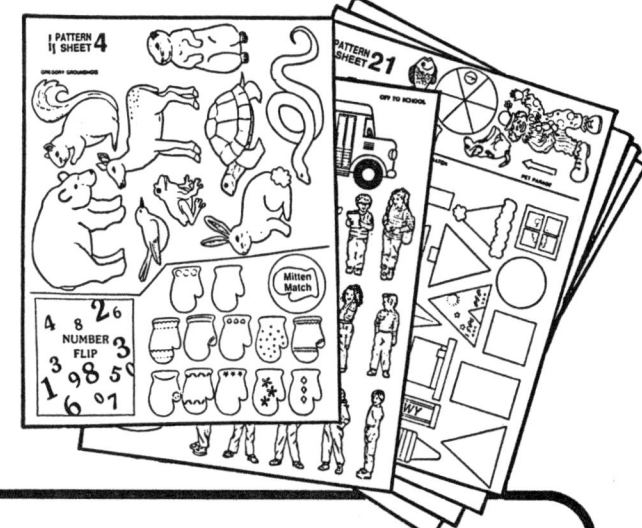

FOR YOUR ORDER

NAME:

ADDRESS:

CITY:

STATE: ZIP:

AVAILABLE FROM BOOKSTORES
SCHOOL SUPPLY STORES
OR ORDER DIRECTLY FROM:

building Blocks

38W567 Brindlewood, Elgin, Illinois 60123
708-742-1013   800-233-2448   708-742-1054(FAX)

QTY.		EACH	TOTAL
___	BUILDING BLOCKS Subscription	20.00	___
___	CIRCLE TIME BOOK - HOLIDAYS	9.95	___
___	CLASSROOM PARTIES	8.95	___
___	EVERYDAY BULLETIN BOARDS	8.95	___
___	EVERYDAY CIRCLE TIMES	14.95	___
___	EXPLORING ART	16.95	___
___	FELT BOARD FUN	14.95	___
___	GIFTS, CARDS, AND WRAPS	7.95	___
___	IMAGINATION STRETCHERS	6.95	___
___	LEARNING CENTERS	16.95	___
___	MAKE-TAKE GAMES	12.95	___
___	MAKE-TAKE PATTERN SET	24.95	___
___	PARACHUTE PLAY	7.95	___
___	PARENT PROGRAMS/OPEN HOUSES	9.95	___
___	YEARFUL OF CIRCLE TIMES	14.95	___

TOTAL _____